Twenty Years on

Or, Itinerating in West Virginia

W. M. Weekley

Alpha Editions

This edition published in 2024

ISBN : 9789362516442

Design and Setting By
Alpha Editions
www.alphaedis.com
Email - info@alphaedis.com

As per information held with us this book is in Public Domain. This book is a reproduction of an important historical work. Alpha Editions uses the best technology to reproduce historical work in the same manner it was first published to preserve its original nature. Any marks or number seen are left intentionally to preserve its true form.

Contents

PREFACE ....- 1 -
INTRODUCTION ....- 3 -
CHAPTER I. ....- 6 -
CHAPTER II. ....- 12 -
CHAPTER III. ....- 20 -
CHAPTER IV. ....- 27 -
CHAPTER V. ....- 33 -
CHAPTER VI. ....- 41 -
CHAPTER VII. ....- 47 -
CHAPTER VIII. ....- 57 -

PREFACE

It was not my purpose, in the preparation of this little volume, to make it an autobiography, but rather a narration of incidents connected with the twenty years of humble service which I tried to render the United Brethren Church among the mountains of West Virginia.

These incidents present an all-round view, in outline, of the real life and labors of the itinerant preacher, a third of a century ago, in an isolated section, where the most simple and primitive customs prevailed.

While some of the things related will doubtless amuse the reader, others, I trust, will lead to thoughtful reflection, and carry with them lessons inspiring and helpful. The introduction should first be carefully read by those who expect to be profited by a perusal of the pages which follow. That good may come to the church, and glory to our Redeemer through this unpretentious publication is the prayer of its

AUTHOR.

Kansas City, Mo., May 1, 1907.

I have examined the manuscript of "Twenty Years on Horseback, or Itinerating in West Virginia," and cheerfully submit this note of commendation.

The author, Bishop W. M. Weekley, D.D., I have known for more than thirty years. He entered the ministry when young, with an undivided heart and determined purpose. During the years he served the Church in that State he traveled over almost the entire territory of the West Virginia Conference. The country then was extremely primitive; but simple as the mode of life was at that time, the field was an interesting, even an enjoyable one for a minister who could endure hardness as a good soldier of Christ. I am acquainted with nearly all the sections of the State referred to, and am therefore familiar with many of the places, facts, and persons mentioned, and can assure the reader that the author has given a faithful account of these in his book. No statement is overdrawn or warped for the sake of effect.

W. W. RYMER.

Columbus, Ohio, May 3, 1907.

An examination of the following pages caused me to live my early life over again. Having spent twenty-three years in the ministry within the bounds of the West Virginia Conference, and having been intimately associated with the author of this volume during the most of that period, I am very familiar with many of the places, persons, and events mentioned, and can testify to the correctness of the record he makes, and to the faithfulness of the pictures drawn. This book will stir the thoughts and rekindle the fire within the old itinerants, and, as well, I trust, arouse the young to larger activities in soul winning.

R. A. HITT.

Chillicothe, Ohio, May 4, 1907.

The author of this book and myself were boys together. We were born and reared within four miles of each other, were converted in the same church, and for years were members of the same Sunday school and congregation. We were licensed to preach on the same charge, and spent the earlier years of our ministry in the same conference together. In many instances we traveled the same roads, preached in the same communities, and mingled with the same people.

After having examined the contents of this volume in manuscript form, I am sure it contains a faithful description of the varied conditions which made up the life and experiences of the United Brethren itinerant minister of that time among the hills and mountains of West Virginia.

A. ORR.

Circleville, Ohio, April 30, 1907.

INTRODUCTION

The past lives through the printed page. The ages would be blank if books were not made recording the events and achievements of men. No form of history is more interesting and profitable than that which recites the career of those who, obedient to their divine commission, proclaimed to fellowmen the sweet message of Christ's redeeming love. The completeness of their consecration, their undaunted courage and persistency in the face of many difficulties, and their marvelous success evidence in them the presence of superhuman power. It is the genius of Christianity to inspire and develop the unselfish and heroic in men. The splendid specimens of self-sacrifice and moral courage, which adorn the pages of Christian literature, charm the reader and inspire him to more Christlike endeavor. These life-stories constitute a rich, priceless legacy for present and future generations.

In this admirable volume, Bishop Weekley has modestly removed the curtain from twenty years of his own strenuous ministerial life spent in the mountains and valleys of West Virginia, and given the reader a conception of what it meant to lift up the Christ and extend his kingdom in that rugged region. The book is biographical in character, but since "biography is the soul of history," it is history in reality. The scenes and events which he presents suggest the character of the work which others had to do in laying the foundations of our Church in those sections.

It would be difficult to find more striking examples of Christian altruism and heroism anywhere in this country than the godly men who preached the gospel among the mountains and in the valleys of the Virginias in the early years of our denominational history. These men embodied those elements of character and graces of the Spirit which are essential to success in Christian work anywhere. Having heard the call of God, and having felt the spell of the divine spirit, they yielded themselves unreservedly to the gospel ministry. They possessed strength of conviction, singleness of aim, earnestness of purpose, and concentration of effort. As a rule these pioneer preachers had but one business—that of the King. They were so absorbed in the saving of men and women, and in extending the kingdom, that they gave but little attention to present physical comforts and future needs. Many of them were without property, and when they sang,

> "No foot of land do I possess,
>
> No cottage in this wilderness,"

there was a literalness about it which would have dismayed men of less faith and consecration. Without seeking to enrich themselves in material things they labored earnestly to bring the spiritual riches of heaven to the hearts and homes of others.

They were busy men—men of action. They omitted no opportunities to do good. Intervals of rest were few and far between. The modern minister's vacation was to them unknown. They met their "appointments" with surprising regularity. Neither storm, nor distance, nor weariness thwarted their plans. Their announcements were always made conditionally—"no preventing providence"—but they never calculated for providence to prevent them being on hand at the appointed place and hour. The strain of toil was constant, but their iron resolution, and the work itself, proved a strong tonic. The success of one service was inspiration for the next. Visiting from house to house, exhorting the people to faithful Christian living, distributing religious literature, and preaching week days as well as Sundays made their lives full of heavy tasks, all of which were performed with happy hearts. They possessed the glowing and tireless zeal of the preaching friars of the Middle Ages, and with many of them the clear flame of their zeal was undimmed until the fire was turned to ashes.

They were men of thought as well as action. Their preparation was made in the college of experience, in which they proved themselves apt students. They studied few books and only the best. They cultivated and practised the perilous art of reading on horseback. They pored over books and papers in humble homes by flickering candle or pine-knot light long after the family had retired. It is remarkable what extended knowledge of the English Scriptures, methods of sermonizing, oratorical style and forceful delivery these men acquired. They knew well, and by that surest form of knowledge—the knowledge born of verified experience—all they proclaimed in message to the people. There was freshness of thought, aptness of illustration, and forcefulness of expression that was native to them. The majestic forms of nature in the regions where they toiled inspired in them the sublimest thoughts of God and his eternal truth. The marvelous results of the sermons of such men as Markwood, Glossbrenner, Bachtel, Warner, Nelson, Graham, Howe, Hott, and others proved them great preachers in the highest and truest sense.

They were men of tact as well as thought, and adjusted themselves to the conditions. They preached wherever the people would assemble—in leafy grove, by the river bank, in the humble home, in the log schoolhouse, in the village hall, in the vacant storeroom, and in the unpretentious church-house. They did not always have the exhilarating and inspirational effect of great crowds, but they preached "in demonstration of the Spirit," kindling the deepest emotions in their hearers, often arousing them to tremendous intensity and causing waves of overpowering feeling to sweep over them. Saints shouted the praises of God and penitents pleaded for mercy. These heralds of the Cross employed none of the familiar devices of modern times for securing crowds and reaching results. There were no specially-prepared and widely-scattered handbills, no local advertising committees, no daily newspapers with flashing headlines and portraits, no great choral or orchestral attractions. What made these fallible men so forceful and successful in winning others? The explanation lies in the fact of their spiritual enduement. They wrought in the name of Christ and under the influence of the Holy Spirit.

In no portion of our Zion have ministers made stronger and more lasting impression upon the people. Whenever present in a home they were the guests of honor. Their strong personalities and noble traits of character, as well as their calling itself, won for them the esteem of old and young. Parents named their children after them, and exhorted their sons to find in them their models for manhood. In thus honoring these noblemen of God they exalted the work of the ministry in the minds of the young, and prepared the way for the Lord to call them into his service. This may account, at least in part, for the great number who have gone into the ministry from these mountain districts.

Let no one fancy that somber shadows rested continually upon the pathway of these ministers. There was a joyous side to their ministerial life. When together as a class, or among their parishioners, their stories and jokes were abundant, spontaneous, and of the purest type. When they met at institutes, camp-meetings, and conferences they enjoyed one round of good cheer and solid comfort. Their services of song drowned all dull cares. Their lives had shadows, but they refreshed themselves in the rifts and glorious sunbursts.

The people to whom these men of God proclaimed the gospel were not, as a rule, rich in material things, but they possessed great hearts, in which love and kindness flowed as pure and refreshing as the streams of water that rippled down the mountain side.

We rejoice that Bishop Weekley has given to the Church this book. Many aged ministers, who once toiled in the Virginias, will live over again the scenes of their lives as they read these pages. Young men will be stimulated to more earnest endeavor as they learn of the hardships and complete consecration of God's servants in pioneer days. No one will weary in reading this excellent volume. The good Bishop has written in harmony with an established sentiment in book-making—"it is the chief of all perfections in books to be plain and brief."

W. O. FRIES.

Dayton, Ohio.

CHAPTER I.

The Virginias have turned out more United Brethren preachers, perhaps, than any other section of the same size between the oceans. These pulpiteers have ranged in the scale of ability and efficiency from A to Z. Some achieved distinction in one way and another; others, though faithful and useful, were little known beyond their conference borders. Nor have all remained among the mountains. Dozens and scores of them have gone out into other parts of the Church. At this writing they are to be found in no less than nineteen different conferences, and, as a class, they are not excelled by any in devotion to the Church, in unremitting toil, and in spiritual fervor and downright enthusiasm. Some—many who spent their lives in building up the Zion of their choice among the Virginia hills, have gone to glory. Among these heroes I may mention J. Markwood, J. J. Glossbrenner, Z. Warner, J. Bachtel, J. W. Perry, J. W. Howe, S. J. Graham, I. K. Statton, and J. W. Hott. Other names, perhaps not so illustrious, but just as worthy, are to be found in God's unerring record. The historian will never tell all about them. Their labors, sacrifices, and sufferings will never be portrayed by any human tongue, no matter how eloquent, or by any pen, however versatile and fruitful it may be. Footsore and weary, dust covered and battle scarred, they reached the end of their pilgrimage and heard heaven's "well done." What a blessed legacy they bequeathed to their sons and daughters in the gospel!

"Old Virginia" was, in part, the field chosen by Otterbein himself, and by his devout colaborers. This was more than a hundred years ago. In 1858 the Parkersburg, now West Virginia Conference, was organized out of that part of the mother conference lying west of the Alleghanies—a territory three hundred miles long, roughly speaking, by two hundred in width. In its physical aspects the country is exceedingly rough, and difficult of travel. But the people, though mostly rural in their customs and mode of living, and many of them poor, so far as this world's goods are concerned, are warm hearted, genial, and hospitable. When a preacher goes to fill an appointment among "mountaineers," he is not troubled with the thought that perhaps nobody will offer him lodging, or willingly share with him the bounties of his table. I have found things different in other parts of the country.

W. M. WEEKLEY, Twenty Years of Age
Traveling Circuit

The new conference was organized at Centerville, in Tyler County, by Bishop Glossbrenner, in the month of March. Only a few ministers were present, but they were brave and good, ready to do, and, if need be, to die for their Lord. Five miles from this historic place the writer was born on the eighteenth day of September, 1851.

My parents, though poor, were honest and honorable, and toiled unceasingly to provide for and rear in respectability their ten children, of whom I was the oldest.

The neighborhood was far above the average in its religious life and moral worth. A man under the influence of liquor was seldom seen, and a profane word was hardly ever heard. The United Brethren Church was by far the leading denomination in all that country. The old log church in which we all worshiped stood on father's farm, and our home was the stopping-place not only of preachers, but of many others who attended divine service. At times our house was so crowded that mother was compelled to make beds on the floor for the family, and not unfrequently for others as well. But to her it was a great joy to perform such a ministry for the gospel's sake. Her loving hands could always provide for others, no matter who they were, or how many. For the third of a century father was the Sunday-school superintendent in the neighborhood, and, for a longer period, teacher of the juvenile class. Thus he saw little children pass up into other and older classes, and finally to manhood and womanhood, when by and by their children came in and were given a place in "Uncle Dan's" class.

At the age of fourteen I was born the second time, and united with the Church. The occasion was a great revival held by Rev. S. J. Graham, of precious memory. Seeing my oldest sister, Sarah, bow at the altar, greatly moved my young heart. A few moments later I observed father coming back toward the door, and thinking perhaps he was wanting to speak to me on the subject of religion, I immediately left the house. My state of mind became awful. The next evening I saw mother pressing her way toward me through the standing crowd. I knew what it meant, and sat down with the hope of concealing myself from her; but how vain the effort! What child ever hid himself away from a mother's love? Putting her hand on my head, she said, "William, won't you be a Christian?" I made no reply, but said to myself, "I can't stand this; I must do something." How her appeal, plaintive and tender, made me weep! It was really the first time she had ever come to me with such directness and warmth of heart. To this very moment I can feel the touch of her hand and hear her loving appeal. The next day I talked with other boys who were with me in school, and asked them to accompany me to the "mourner's bench," which they did.

At that time the class, though in the country, numbered one hundred and seventy souls. Three months later, I was appointed one of its stewards, and with this office came my first experience in raising money for the Church.

The next year I was elected assistant class-leader, and though young and inexperienced, I rendered the very best service I possibly could.

My educational advantages up to this time had been only such as the common schools afforded, with the addition of a close application to study at the home fireside, aided by the historic "pine torch" and "tallow candle."

From the day of my conversion I could not escape the thought of preaching. The duty of being a Christian was never set before me more forcibly and clearly than was the duty of preaching; but I hesitated. My ignorance, and lack of fitness otherwise for such a high calling, appeared as insurmountable barriers. I could not understand why God should pass by others, better in heart and far more capable, and choose me. So the struggle went on. In the mean time I began to read such books as I could secure. The Bible, "Smith's Bible Dictionary," and "Dick's Works," constituted my library. The last named was rather heavy for a lad only in his teens, but I rather enjoyed such studies. The first book I ever purchased was "Religious Emblems," which proved exceedingly helpful to my young life.

When seventeen I preached my first sermon, or, perhaps I should say, made my first public effort. It was in an old log church on Little Flint Run, in Doddridge County. Brother Christopher Davis, a local preacher, was holding a meeting, and at the close of the morning services announced that I would preach at night. What a day that was to me! How I tried to think and pray!

When I reached the church I found it full, with many standing in the aisle about the door. I felt so unprepared—so utterly helpless—that I immediately retired to a secret place, where I again besought the Lord for help. Returning, I started in with the preliminaries, but was badly scared. No man can describe his feelings under such circumstances. Many a preacher who scans these pages will appreciate my situation. I spent a good part of the first fifteen minutes mopping my face. I seemed to be in a sweat-box; but by the time I reached my sermon, or whatever it might be called, the embarrassment was all gone. I still remember the text: "And I will bring you into the land concerning the which I did swear to give it to Abraham, to Isaac, and to Jacob; and I will give it you for an heritage. I am the Lord." It was immense; but the most of young preachers begin just that way. At this distance from the occasion, I do not recall anything I said, and am glad I cannot. However, there was one redeeming feature about the effort, and that was its brevity. In twenty minutes I had told all I knew, and perhaps more. I have never been able to understand why the people listened so patiently. They really seemed to be interested, but why, or in what, I have never known. I have not tried that text since, and I do not think I ever shall. It is too profound to even think of as the basis of a discourse to common people.

Dr. J. L. Hensley, when pastor of Middle Island Circuit, early in the sixties, had a somewhat singular experience in this same log church. While preaching one Sabbath morning in midsummer from the text, "The seed of the woman shall bruise the serpent's head," the people at his left suddenly became excited, and looking around quickly for the cause, he observed a snake, about two feet long, crawling in a crevice of the wall near the pulpit. Reaching for his hickory cane, which he always carried, he dealt the wily creature a blow which brought it tumbling to the floor, remarking at the same time, "The seed of the woman shall bruise the serpent's head." Thus in the midst of his discourse he was furnished an illustration which made a profound impression upon his hearers, and aided greatly in bringing the truth home to their hearts.

The presiding elder, Rev. S. J. Graham, my spiritual father, by authority of a quarterly conference held at the Long Run appointment, October 23, 1869, gave me a permit to exercise in public for three months. Shortly after this I was prostrated with lung fever, which soon developed the most alarming aspects. Though the ailment was outgeneraled, the process of recovery was slow. In fact, one of my lungs was so impaired that consumption was feared. A noted physician, after carefully diagnosing my case, frankly told me that nothing could be done for my lung; but I did not believe a word he told me. I had decided that I would make preaching my life work, and believed that God would give me a chance to try it. It might be noted here that ten years later this same doctor was in his grave, while I was a better specimen of physical manhood than he ever was.

"Commit thy way unto the Lord; trust also in him, and he shall bring it to pass." What will he bring to pass? The right thing, and in the right way. Such has been my observation and experience in all the years that have come and gone since the hand of affliction was so keenly felt.

December 25, 1869, I was granted quarterly conference license in a regular way, and attended the annual conference which met in Hartford City, Mason County, the following March. Much of the time while there I was not able to walk from my stopping-place to the church, though not a half dozen blocks distant. Some of the brethren feared that I would not live to get back home again. But I wanted a circuit. With that end in view I had gone to conference, and no amount of persuasion could turn me aside from the one great purpose that had taken complete possession of my soul. I was entering the work with a full knowledge of what it meant. I had heard the brethren talk of their privations and abundant labors, and, as well, of their victories and joy of heart. The report of the year then closing was most suggestive. The eighteen fields of the conference contained one hundred and sixty-seven preaching places, and had paid twenty-four men a little less than $140 each upon an average, not counting outside gifts. West Columbia Circuit paid its two pastors, Revs. W. B. Hodge and I. M. Underwood, $400. The next highest was $339.19, and was paid the brace of pastors who served the Glenville charge—Revs. W. W. Knipple and Elias Barnard. The other sixteen pastorates ranged from $267.15 down to $35, the last named amount having been received by Rev. J. W. Boggess, on Hessville Mission. The Parkersburg District paid Elder Graham $227.87, while West Columbia District only reached $152.85 for its superintendent, Rev. J. W. Perry. To the support of each of the districts, however, the parent missionary board added $100.

When the Stationing Committee reported, my name was read out as the junior preacher for Philippi Circuit, with Rev. A. L. Moore, pastor in charge. This appointment was given, as more than one assured me in later years, simply to satisfy my mind. No one expected me to go to it. As the field already had a man, my failure to reach it would make no difference in any way.

Returning home I told father what had been done, and that I must have the necessary outfit for a circuit-rider; namely, a horse, a saddle and bridle, and a pair of saddle-bags. No matter what else a man had, or did not have, in those days, these things were essential to efficiency among the mountains of West Virginia.

At once I began preparations for leaving home. Mother was thoughtful enough to make me a pair of leggings which buttoned up at the sides and reached above the knees. No one article made with hands was ever more valuable to a Virginia itinerant than leggings.

Philippi Circuit was seventy-five miles distant among the mountains, and would require, owing to the bad roads, two and a half days of hard travel on horseback to reach it. At the appointed time, April 11, 1870, early in the morning, I rode out of the old lane and up the hillside. All I had of earthly possessions was in my saddle-bags. One end contained my library, (Bible, Hymn-book, "Smith's Bible Dictionary," "Binney's Theological Compend," "Religious Emblems," and one volume of "Watson's Institutes,") while in the other was stored my wardrobe, scant and plain. When far up on the side of the hill I looked back and saw mother standing on the porch. She had not ceased to watch me from the moment I started. Tears unbidden filled my eyes, and with these came an appreciation of our home that I had never experienced before. The home had been humble, to be sure, but it was Christian. We had a family altar, from which the sweet incense of prayer ascended daily to God. I could truthfully say:

"Jesus, I my cross have taken,

All to leave and follow thee."

A mile distant I joined, by a prearranged plan, Rev. G. W. Weekley, my uncle, and Rev. Isaac Davis, both of whom were also en route to their distant fields of toil.

At the end of the second day we reached Glady Fork, on Lewis Circuit, where my uncle lived. How weary after so long a ride! At that time my health was still so precarious, and my strength so limited, that I could not walk a hundred yards up grade without resting. To dismount from my horse, open and close a gate, and then get back into the saddle, exhausted me. Remaining over a few days with my uncle, I tried to preach on Sunday morning, but found myself exhausted at the end of twenty-four minutes. In a few days, however, I was sufficiently rested from my long ride to journey on to my own circuit, where I soon found the preacher in charge, and plans were discussed for the year's work. This was historic ground. It was an old United Brethren field, having been traveled by Statton, Stickley, Warner, Hensley, and others, in the late fifties and early sixties, when it included twenty or more preaching-places, spread over portions of several counties.

CHAPTER II.

Philippi Circuit contained at this time the following appointments: Romines Mills, Gnatty Creek, Peck's Run, Indian Fork, Mt. Hebron, Green Brier, and Zeb's Creek. Later I added two more—one on Big Run, and the other on Brushy Fort, at the home of "Mother" Simons. Two of the preaching places lay "beyond" the Middle Fork River—a rolling, dashing stream, fresh from the mountains, and at times dangerous to cross. It was so clear that a silver piece the size of a quarter could be seen at a depth of several feet. The first time I attempted to ford it I put my life in jeopardy. Because the bottom could be seen distinctly, I imagined it was not deep, but after a few paces I was in mid-side to my horse, and going deeper every step. Perceiving the danger I was in, I tried to turn my horse about, and did so only after the greatest effort, owing to the almost irresistible current which was gradually bearing horse and rider downward. Going to a house near by I made some inquiry about the stream, and was told that if I had gone ten feet farther I should have been swept away by the swift running waters. How grateful I was to God for the deliverance. During the following winter my life was endangered by floating ice at the same crossing-place. Brother Moore about the same time, perhaps a little later, seeing he could not ford the stream, decided to lead his horse across the ice at a point below the regular crossing, where there was but little current; but when twenty feet from the shore toward which he was headed, the ice gave way, and the faithful animal went under. Having hold of the bridle rein, however, he managed to keep his head above the water until a passage way was broken through to dry land.

One instinctively shudders as he recalls the dangers which at times thrust themselves suddenly across the pathway of the early preachers of the Virginia and Parkersburg conferences when the fields were so large and travel so excessive. Brother Moore informed me, as we looked over the charge, that I would have to take the "outsiders" for my support, as the circuit only paid $300, and he could not get along on less and pay rent. It struck me that he was about right, so I readily agreed to his proposition. Then what? Well, at each preaching place I found a "sinner" who agreed to serve as my steward, and these men did well, everything considered. For the year I received $97, including an overcoat and several pairs of yarn socks.

At one of the appointments an unfortunate episode occurred over my salary. The steward one day stepped over the line, and got after some of the church-members for money. He very well knew they were abundantly able to help, but they flatly refused. This so upset him, so I was told, that he expressed his opinion of them in language far more vigorous than polite. It is a joy, however, to note in this connection that some of these stewards soon became Christians, and active helpers in the Church.

Out of the pittance I received, possibly all, or more than I was worth, I added to my little library, which could easily be put in one end of my saddle-bags when I left home, the following books: "Bible Not of Man," "Conversation of Jesus," "Jesus on the Holy Mount," "Pilgrim's Progress," "Dying Thoughts," "Bible Text Book," "Jacobus on John," "God's Word Written," "Paley's Theology," "Our Lord's Parables," "Webster's Dictionary," "Bible True," "Rock of Our Salvation," "Companion to the Bible," "Dictionary of the Bible," "Credo," "Rise and Progress of Religion in the Soul," and "Hand of God in History." This, of course, was not a lavish purchase of books, but it did pretty well for one with a cash income of not more than $75.

We had some good revivals that year. Ninety-nine were received into church fellowship, while many more were converted. At Indian Fork we held meeting in a little log cabin, about twenty feet square, with a great fire-place in one side. It is surprising to see how many people can be crowded into so small a place when they are anxious to attend a revival. Night after night for weeks this little room was packed like a sardine case. But the outcome was glorious. Some of the best citizens of the community were reached and won to Christ.

After a few services were held, and it was seen how insufficient the little room was to accommodate the many who wanted to come, we put on foot the project of building a church, and immediately set about the work. The plan was so unique that the whole neighborhood became interested. Some felled trees; others "scored and hewed" the logs; those who had teams volunteered to haul them, while others still made shingles, or helped with the foundation; "for the people had a mind to work." Before the meetings closed the house was up and ready for use—an edifice which served as a place of worship for many years.

The people all over the circuit were kind and forbearing, and greatly encouraged me by waiting on my ministry, and hearing what little I had to say. I visited all classes of persons, rich and poor, and had all kinds of experiences. In some homes I enjoyed the hospitality offered; in others it was not so highly enjoyed, but keenly appreciated. At one of the preaching points a certain brother insisted upon my going home with him for dinner after the morning service, which I consented to do. It was a rainy day. He lived in a cabin of one room on the hillside. On either side of the dwelling was a shed. Under one of these he kept his corn; under the other, where we entered the house, the hogs slept and the chickens roosted. His only piece of regular furniture was a chair. As to where and when he got it I did not inquire. Long poles reaching across the room and fastened to the walls, with a forked stick under them in the center, constituted a kind of double bedstead. When I entered the door I observed a large "feather tick" piled upon these poles. Finally, something moved under it, and then a boy of ten or twelve summers, almost suffocated, crawled out and made for the door. His purpose, no doubt, was to hide from the preacher when he saw him coming, but finding he could not get his breath, decided to retreat to another place of concealment where there was more fresh air. I did not eat much dinner. I told "mine host" that I was not hungry, and, in fact, was not. They had only a broken skillet in which to bake bread, fry meat, and "make gravy." As soon as possible I excused myself, and started for my next appointment. Indeed, I was glad I had another one that day.

Many other amusing incidents occurred during the year. These always find a place in the itinerant's life, and it is well, perhaps, that they do, as they offset in a measure his somber experiences. I am frank to confess that it is easy for me to see the funny side of a happening, if it has one, and to enjoy a joke though it be on myself.

In the early days of the West Virginia Conference, what was known as the "plug hat" was much in evidence among preachers. Such "headwear" was a distinguishing mark, hence no circuit-rider with proper self-respect, or wishing to give tone to his calling, could afford to don anything else. Being young, and somewhat ambitious to hold up the ministerial standard, at least in appearance, I determined to secure one as soon as I could get a few dollars ahead. However, the way opened for the gratification of my wish sooner than I had expected. Brother Moses Simons had one he didn't care to wear, so I bantered him for a trade. It was in first-class condition, but entirely too large for me. Even after putting a roll of paper around under the lining, it came down nearly to my ears. What was I to do? I must have a high-topped hat, but was not able to purchase a new one. At last I decided to wear it, if my ears did occasionally protest against its close proximity to them. It distinguished me from common people for the next two years, and so answered well its purpose.

One day as I was riding up a little creek between two high hills I passed a group of urchins who evidently were unused to preachers. They watched me in utter silence till I had passed them a few yards, when one of them piped out, "Lord, what a hat." No doubt they had an interesting story to relate to their parents when they returned to their humble cabin home.

Not long after this I met a gentleman, so-called, in the road, and bade him the time of day, as was my custom. He returned the salutation with, "How are you, hat?" and passed on without another word. To me this was exceedingly offensive, for I was sure there was something in and under the hat, and any such remark was an uncalled-for reflection upon my dignity and the high calling I represented. I did not know the man, and to the best of my knowledge have never seen him since, but to this day, though removed from the event more than a third of a century, I harbor the thought that if I ever do run across him I shall demand some sort of reparation for the insult.

The annual conference met in Pennsboro, Bishop Weaver presiding. During the year I had improved much in health, owing to my horseback exercise and the great amount of singing I did, which doubtless had much to do with the development of lung muscle.

At conference I went before the committee on applicants with eight others, five of whom were referred back to their respective quarterly conferences for further preparation. For some reason the examination was unusually critical. One question propounded to each was, "Do you seek admission into the conference simply to vote for a presiding elder?" There was some doubt in my case on a doctrinal point, according to the report of the chairman, Rev. W. Slaughter, an erratic old brother. He said the boy was all right, except "a little foggy on depravity." Possibly I was, for I didn't think much of that portion of our creed. However, I see more in it, and of it, after all these years, than I did then. In the light of my observations and experiences with men, I am not inclined to deny the doctrine.

I was appointed by this conference to Lewis Circuit, an old, run down field, embracing parts of three counties. Rev. Isaac Davis was sent along as a helper "in the Lord." We had grown up together in the same neighborhood, and were members of the same congregation. He was a young man of sterling moral qualities, and proved himself a loyal and valuable coworker.

After spending a few days with our parents and friends, we started, early in April, for the scene of toil to which we had been assigned for the year. From the day we left home we ceased not to pray that the Lord of the harvest would give us at least one hundred souls as trophies of his grace, and to that end we labored constantly.

We found the following regular appointments: Glady Fork, Hinkleville, Union Hill, Little Skin Creek, White Oak, Waterloo, Indian Camp, Walkersville, Braxton, and Centerville. Soon we added two more, namely, Bear Run and Laurel Run. The charge agreed to pay us $210, but fell a little short, reaching only $170. Of this I received $90, and Brother Davis the remaining $80. The assessment for missions was $25, and about $10 for other purposes, which we regarded as a pretty high tax for benevolences. Yet the entire amount was raised after a most vigorous and thorough canvass of all the appointments. As I now remember, no one gave more than twenty-five cents.

Our protracted meetings lasted more than six months, and resulted in the reception of one hundred and one persons into church fellowship. While in the revival at Hinkleville, a great shout occurred one night over the conversion of some far-famed sinners, during which the floor of the church gave way and went down some two feet. Before dismissing the people, I announced that we would meet and make repairs the next day. At the appointed time it seemed that nearly all the men and boys in the country round about were on hand, ready to render what service they could in repairing the house of the Lord.

This was a revival of far-reaching influence. The country for miles around was thoroughly stirred. One of the leading men became interested one night, and decided upon a new life. As he approached the church the next day he heard us singing what was then a very popular song—"Will the Angels Come?" The words and melody fairly charmed him, and kindled new hope in a life that had been given over to sin. As he opened the church door, the key of faith opened his heart's door to the Savior, and he rushed down the aisle to tell us of his wonderful experience. It was all victory that morning. The conversion of such a man profoundly affected the people, and led to many more decisions for Christ.

During this meeting my colleague arose one evening to preach. As he had the test, with book, chapter, and verse all by heart, he did not open his Bible, but began by saying, "You will find my text in Revelation, third chapter, and twentieth verse." Just then an apple fell through a hole in his coat-pocket on to the floor. As he stooped to pick it up, another fell out. Returning them to his pocket, he again started—"Revelation, third chapter and twentieth verse," when suddenly the two restless apples dropped out again. After picking them up, he started in the third time, "You will find my text in,"—but all was gone. He couldn't even think of Revelation. The audience was at the point of roaring, so in the midst of his confusion he turned to me and said, "Brother Weekley, what is my text? I don't know what nor where it is." I answered, "Behold, I stand at the door and knock." "Yes, yes," he said, "I remember it now," and proceeded with his discourse, but did not recover that evening from the knock-out blow he had received.

Preaching through such a long revival campaign was no easy thing, when I had only a few sermons in stock, and these were all "home made." I think the material in them was all right, but the mechanical construction was not according to any particular rule. I endeavored to give my hearers plenty to eat, but I did not understand how to serve the food in courses. It was like putting a lot of hominy, and pork, and cabbage, and beans into the same dish, and saying to the people, "Here it is; help yourselves." But as a few sermons could not be made to last indefinitely, I was compelled to apply myself to study, no little of which was done on horseback. Every itinerant in West

Virginia at that time had to do the same thing. While this method of study was not the most desirable, it nevertheless had its redeeming features. Ofttimes, after riding a dozen or fifteen miles over rough, hilly roads, I would alight, hitch my horse, and while the weary animal was resting, mount a log near by and practice to my heart's content the sermon I was preparing for my next appointment. Again and again did I make the welkin ring as I preached to an audience of great trees about me. Does this appear amusing to the reader? Do you doubt that such experiences ever occurred? If so, ask some of the earlier preachers of the conference who are yet living if they ever did such a thing while circuit-riding among the mountains.

Did we ever feel lonesome as we traversed the forests or climbed the hills? Not for a moment. It was an inspiring place to be. The birds sing so sweetly there. The gurgling, murmuring streamlets are ever musical as they steal their way along through gulches, over their rocky beds. The scenery is sublime. Nature's book stands wide open, and abounds with richest lessons and illustrations. No wonder Glossbrenner and Markwood, Warner and Howe, with a host of others, could preach! The very mountains amid which they were born and reared conspired to make them lofty characters, and majestic in their pulpit efforts. While Union Biblical Seminary, and our colleges generally, are grand, helpful schools, let it not be forgotten that "Brush College" is not without its advantages, and should be given due credit for the inspiration and rugged manliness it imparts to its students.

My home this year was with Brother James Hull, on the headwaters of French Creek, fully forty miles from the nearest railroad station. Mother Hull was one of God's noble women. She professed sanctification, and lived it every day. I can never forget her helpfulness to me, a mere child in years and service. I must see her in heaven.

If I returned home after each Sabbath's work, it required one hundred and fifty miles travel to make one round of the circuit. My associate also had a good home on another part of the charge; but unfortunately for him, and for some others as well, his zeal led him into trouble. Brother Mike Boyles, with whom he stayed, was a good, true man, and was ever delighted to have a preacher with him. One Sunday he went to see a friend a few miles distant, and innocently carried home on his horse a large, nice, well-matured pumpkin. His purpose, no doubt, was to prepare a special dish for his guest; but his preacher was not pleased with such an infraction of the Sabbath law. A short while after this he discoursed in the neighborhood church on the text, "I stand in doubt of you." Among other things, he said he stood in doubt of a church-member who would go visiting on Sunday and carry "pumpkins" home with him. Brother Boyles very naturally made the application a personal one, and ever afterward refused to be reconciled.

During the year I married two couples. One of the men was a horse buyer, and was considered "away up" financially. Of course I expected no insignificant sum for my services; it ought to have been ten dollars or more; but let the reader imagine, if he can, my disappointment, if not disgust, when he handed me forty cents in "shinplasters." By "shinplasters" I mean a certain kind of currency which circulated during our civil strife in the early sixties, in the form of five, ten, twenty-five and fifty cent certificates.

Speaking of this wedding recalls the fact that it was on this circuit, while visiting my uncle the year before, that I married my first couple. I remember, too, that I approached the occasion with great trepidation. It was an awful task. But the eventful hour finally came. The parsonage, so called, where the nuptials were to be celebrated, was a log cabin of one room. The kitchen, which stood several feet from the main building, was the only place offered in which to arrange the toilet. At last I stood before the young couple and began the ceremony, which I had committed to memory. Yes, I had it sure, as I thought. I had gone over it twenty times or more. In practising for the occasion I had joined trees and fence stakes, and I know not what all, together; but at the very moment when I needed it, and couldn't get along without it, the whole thing suddenly left me. There I was. After an extended pause and a most harrowing silence I rallied, and began by saying, "We are gathered together." Just then my voice failed me; it seemed impossible to make a noise, even. I fairly gasped for breath, for that was the one thing I seemed to need most. At last the effort was renewed. How I got through I never knew. I seemed to be in a mysterious realm, where the unknowable becomes more incomprehensible, and when all the past and future seem to unite in the present. Finally I wound up what seemed to be long-drawn out affair, and pronounced the innocent couple man and wife. I am glad they always considered themselves married. I have but little recollection of what I did or said during the ordeal. In fact, I do not care to know, since I am so far away from the occasion. Yes, that was my first wedding.

The year was not without its material enterprises, for we completed the churches at Glady Fork and Waterloo, repaired one at Indian Camp, and started a new one at Laurel Run. Some of these stand yet as moral and religious centers, and, at times, through the intervening years, have been the scenes of great spiritual awakenings.

Conference was held at New Haven, in Mason County, with Bishop D. Edwards in the chair. While our report was thought to be fairly good, I asked for a change, believing that I could do better work on another field. The favor was granted, and Hessville Mission assigned me as my third charge.

At the close of this year there were thirty-one ministers employed in the conference, whose aggregate salary was $4,551.77, or an average of $147 each. The three presiding elders received, all told, $843.83. These figures indicate something of the sacrifices made by the men who gave themselves to the early work of building up the Church in the Virginias. Greater heroism of the apostolic type was never displayed by any of the sons of Otterbein, nor can any part of the country show greater achievements for the work done.

CHAPTER III.

Hessville Mission embraced portions of Harrison and Marion counties, and was made up of the following preaching places: Quaker Fork, Glade Fork, Indian Run, Big Run, Little Bingamon, Ballard School-house, Salt Lick, Plumb Run, and Paw-paw. In all this territory we did not own a single church edifice. By fall I had added Dent's Run, Bee Gum, and Glover's Gap, making twelve appointments in all. At the last named place I held a revival in a union church. The meeting was good, and telling most favorably upon some of the best families of the town, when an unknown miscreant at an early morning hour applied the torch and reduced the building to ashes. All I lost in the conflagration was my Bible and hymn-book. Moving into a schoolhouse near by, the meeting was continued, and a class organized. By the middle of the winter there had been sixty-five accessions, but from that on till spring I had to lay by on account of measles.

At Little Bingamon we had a great meeting. The entire community was deeply stirred. "Aunt Susan" Martin was my main helper and standby. While devout in life, and strong in faith, she had a blunt, honest way of saying things which often amused the people. At this meeting two of her children made a start. One was a son of some fifteen winters. He literally wore himself out by his night and day pleadings at the altar, and became so hoarse that he could scarcely talk. His mother was greatly agitated over his condition, and grew exceedingly anxious to see the intense struggle terminated. One evening she bowed at the altar with him that she might, through instruction, show him a better way. She did not believe that bodily exercise could be made to avail anything in seeking salvation. Finally, for a moment, she lost her patience, and said, "Now, if you don't quit this kind of praying you will kill yourself. Stop it, I tell you, or I'll box your ears good. The Lord isn't deaf, that you should 'holler' so loud." Then turning to her husband who, at the time, was a professed moralist, though faithful in attending and supporting the church services, she said: "George, you ought to be ashamed of yourself. Not a word have you for this poor child. Now come and talk to him. To stand and look on is no way to do."

The dear sister was right, not only in thinking that the father ought to help the son, but in protesting against unnecessary physical demonstrations in seeking religion. It is not the loud praying or constant pleading that saves men, but faith in the world's Redeemer. Rev. H. R. Hess, one of the leading ministers in the West Virginia Conference, was soundly converted and received into the church during this meeting.

What a good home I had while on this charge! Brother Daniel Mason, a father in Israel, whose life was as pure as a sunbeam, took me to his home and heart, and treated me very much as the Shunammite did Elisha. He built me a little room on his porch, and put therein a bed, bookcase, table, and candlestick. The worth of such a place to a young minister is next to incalculable. Twice a day he read the Word and prayed. He was on good terms with his Lord, and talked to him with the greatest assurance. Some of the sweetest memories of my earlier ministry cluster about this Christian home. The fruition of the upper and better life he now enjoys as the reward of his faith, service, and devotion while here below.

The circuit agreed to pay me $100, and kept its contract. The first quarter I received $14.81, the second, $18.35; the third, $17.75; and the last $49.05. The conference added $50, which pushed my support up to $150. With this salary, much above the average for a single man, I could afford to pay $21.50 for a new suit of clothes, and $4 for a new "two-story" silk hat.

On my way to conference a few days were spent with friends in the home neighborhood. Rev. E. Lorenz, father of the music writer, was living and preaching in Parkersburg at this time. He had organized a German congregation, and held services in the lecture-room of our English church. The Committee on Entertainment sent me to stay with him during the conference session which was held in the city. Thoughts of that superlatively Christian home linger with me to this day. I shall never forget how parents and children bowed together in prayer, morning and evening, and how each took part in the devotions. Too much emphasis cannot be placed upon the importance of prayer in the home. Nothing else, on the human side, so anchors the family and builds up character. The fact that the fire has died out on so many domestic altars is, itself, proof that family religion does not receive the attention it once did.

At this conference I was permitted to pass the second and third years' course of reading, which put me in the class to be ordained. I can never blot from memory the prayer offered by the lamented Doctor Warner at the ordination service. He seemed to pour out his very soul in petition to God for the young men being set apart to the work of the ministry. I wept like a child while he thus prayed, and anew pledged to Jesus and the Church the service of my life.

Grafton at this time was constituted a mission station, and made my field for the coming year. The town then (1873) had a population of about three thousand souls, and was located mainly on a steep hillside. In fact, it stands about the same way yet, though containing several thousand more people. We had no church-house, and no organization, though there were a few members scattered through the place. Seventy-five dollars were appropriated by the conference toward my support. A preaching-place called "Old Sandy," some twelve miles distant, was also given me. Here we had a gracious revival.

I later took up two more points—Maple Run and Glade Run—and organized a class at each. At the close of the year these country classes were formed into a separate charge, and became self-supporting.

W. M. WEEKLEY, Thirty Years of Age

Presiding Elder

At Grafton the work progressed slowly, and with some difficulty for a time. A friend gave us, free of charge, the use of a church-house which, by some means, had fallen into his hands. The first thing was to organize a Sabbath school, which started off well. When certain church partisans saw the outlook, they offered to take part in the school, and adroitly got possession of the offices. When I discovered the real situation, I determined to bring the matter of control to an issue, and did. I deliberately stated that I had been sent there to organize a United Brethren Church and Sabbath school, and proposed to carry out my instructions. I was pleased to have teachers and other helpers from sister denominations join in the work, I added, but the school would be reported to my conference. The result is easily imagined. Our friends, so-called, suddenly dropped out, and from that day to this the identity of the school has never been questioned.

The seventy-five dollars appropriated by the conference was about all I received, and twenty-five dollars of that went in a lump to the centennial fund. If a kind family had not taken me in, free of cost, I could not have remained the year through. For the second year the support given was about the same. The third year there were two of us to support, hence a special effort had to be made to increase the pay. Three hundred and twelve dollars was the amount actually received, eighty dollars of which was paid on rent; but we lived well; no such thing as want seemed to be within a thousand leagues of our humble home. We were thankful for cheap furniture and home-made carpet. Yea, more, we were happy. God's ravens carried us our daily portion.

In the early spring of 1875, we began the erection of a chapel which cost, lot and all, $2,800. But a part of it had to be built the second time. Just as the frame was up and ready for roof and siding, a storm passing that way piled it in a promiscuous heap. This occurred on the seventeenth of July. Immediately, however, the work of reconstruction was undertaken, and the edifice was completed in early fall, and dedicated by Doctor Warner. Such experiences try a young man's nerve and purpose, but invariably prove a blessing when the difficulties accompanying them are overcome.

That year I took up an appointment at the Poe School-house, two miles out of town, and organized a class. In those days the preacher was expected to look around for new openings, no matter where he was or how large his field; there is no other way to expand. My criticism of many of our young preachers to-day is that they do not try to enlarge their work. They seem never to look beyond the nest into which the conference settles them. They will live on half salary, and whine about it all year, rather than get out and look up additional territory. Under fair conditions, the young man who is devout and active can secure a good living on any field. Faith and purpose and push will win every time. The year closed with fifty-three members, and ninety-five in the Sunday school.

The conference again convened in Parkersburg, with David Edwards this time as bishop—the last session he ever presided over.

At this period the battle in the Church over the secrecy question was waxing warm. West Virginia had lined up on the liberal side. The bishop, being pronouncedly "anti" in his views, determined to enforce the rules of the Church in the matter of admitting applicants into the conference. A brother who appeared for license was known to belong to some fraternal order, so the good bishop held him up. This brought on a crisis. All was excitement. Some things, it was clear, would have to be settled then and there, and they were. Doctor Warner arose, in the midst of the flurry, and demanded that the young brother be sent to the appropriate committee, which he said was thoroughly competent to deal with the question. The bishop was on his feet also with the fire of determination fairly flashing in his eyes. However, when he fully realized that, with an exception or two, the entire body was against him, he gracefully yielded, thus happily bringing the unfortunate conflict to a close. By morning, matters had again assumed a normal condition, and the bishop kindly requested that all reference to the controversy be expunged from the records.

Notwithstanding Bishop Edwards' somewhat radical position on the secrecy question, he was greatly loved by all our brethren, and by none was his death more sincerely mourned. On Sunday he preached on Elijah's translation; a few days thereafter he was himself translated.

From Grafton I was sent to New Haven circuit, in Mason County, one hundred and sixty miles west. To get there I was compelled to borrow twenty-five dollars. Dr. J. L. Hensley kindly entertained us until a house could be found; for as yet there was not a parsonage in the conference. This was considered one of the best fields we had. The first year it paid me four hundred and sixteen dollars, and the next, four hundred and twenty-seven dollars, with a few presents in the shape of vegetables, groceries, and the like. Of course, I paid rent out of this—thirty-six dollars one year, and fifty the other. I had only four appointments—New Haven, Bachtel, Union, and Vernon, and these were close together. During the two years, one hundred and thirty were received into the Church.

The next conference was held at Bachtel, which gave me my first experience in caring for such a body. Bishop Weaver presided and preached the word mightily on Sunday. He had been popular even since his first visit to that section, in 1870. By request of Hon. George W. Murdock, a wealthy business man in Hartford City, three miles west, he went down there and preached in our church on Sunday evening. Mr. Murdock was an ardent admirer of the bishop. Six years before he had entertained him in his home, and was charmed by him as a preacher and conversationalist. After spending the first hour with him, he slipped into the kitchen and said: "Wife, he is the most wonderful man I ever met. Do come in and hear him talk." The old gentleman never forgot the bishop's sermon on Sunday. For weeks afterward he would talk about it in his store, and elsewhere, sometimes in tears, nearly always ending with the observation, "He is a wonderful man." It might not be out of place to note here that the good bishop more than once shared the benefactions of his wealthy friend.

During my second year on this charge, a peculiar and most trying experience came to our home. A great revival was going on at the Union appointment. The altar was nightly crowded with earnest seekers, some of whom belonged to the best families in the community. Early one morning a young man came hurriedly to the place where I was stopping, and calling me out, said, "Mr. Weekley, I have been sent to tell you that your babe is dead." Hastening home I found the faithful mother watching at the side of the withered flower, and anxiously awaiting my coming. How loving the ministry of friends had been; nor did their tender interest abate a whit until the little lifeless form was put away to sleep in the cemetery on the hillside, in the family lot of Dr. Hensley.

The reader may be anxious to know what I did under the circumstances. There was but one thing to do, that was to seek the guiding hand of duty. Our little one was gone. Just as the thoughtful florist takes his tender plants into their winter quarters before the frost appears, or the chilling winds sweep the plains, so a wise, loving, merciful Father had plucked up the little vine which had rooted itself so thoroughly and deeply in our hearts, and transplanted it in his own heavenly garden. Yes, Charley was safe; so I returned to my meeting with a tender spirit, and the work continued with great power.

More than one preacher who reads this incident will recall the time, or times, when he, too, passed under the cloud, and walked amid the shadows. Again and again I have been made to feel that some people do not sympathize with the minister and his wife, as they do with others, when the death angel tarries and lays his withering hand upon a young life. Somehow they seem to think that the cup, when administered to the preacher's family, is not so bitter— that the thorn does not pierce so deeply. But I know better, and so do a thousand others. It is said of Dr. Daniel Curry, a great man in Methodism in his day, that he was so grieved over the death of his little boy that after returning home from the cemetery he went into the back yard, and observing his little tracks in the sand, got down on his hands and knees and kissed them. Words cannot express my sympathy for the faithful pastor and his family, and my admiration of that faith, devotion, and heroism which in so many instances are necessary to keep them in the work.

Mason County was one of the first fields occupied by the ministers who crossed the Alleghanies westward. Among these were G. W. Statton, J. Bachtel, and Moses Michael. However, prior to this, preaching had been kept up on the Virginia side by pastors of the Scioto Conference. The main one was Jonas Frownfelter, whose name deserves a place alongside the heroes enumerated in the eleventh chapter of Hebrews. On one occasion, when the Ohio River was out of its banks, and too dangerous for the ferryman to venture across, he plunged in a little below the town of Syracuse, swam his horse across, and came out at Hartford City, a half mile below, singing like a conqueror:

"From every stormy wind that blows,

From every swelling tide of woes,

There is a calm, a sure retreat," etc.

All honor to those who put their sweat, and tears, and blood into the foundations of the conference, thus enabling others to build safely and successfully.

Early in the fifties a paper known as the *Virginia Telescope*, was started in West Columbia, ostensibly in the interest of the whole Church, but later developments proved that the object was to organize a Southern United Brethren Church, making the slavery question the basis of the separation. When the presiding elder, G. W. Statton, became aware of its purpose, he threw his official influence against its continuance, and succeeded, by the aid of others, in eliminating it as a disturbing factor.

The reader will pardon me for taking up these early historical threads, woven long before my day as an itinerant, but I have done so with the view to preserving in permanent form interesting facts not generally known, and nowhere written into the history of the Church.

CHAPTER IV.

In March of 1878, the conference assembled in Grafton, with Bishop J. J. Glossbrenner as its presiding officer. At this session the brethren greatly surprised me by electing me one of the presiding elders. No thought of such a thing had ever entered my mind. I could not see the propriety of putting a young man, not yet twenty-seven, over men of age, ability, and experience, hence it was with no little diffidence that I accepted the West Columbia District, in the bounds of which I had already worked two years. The district contained only eleven charges, but these were widely scattered, embracing all or parts of Cabell, Mason, Jackson, Wood, Putnam, Kanawha, and Roane counties, and were as follows: Milton, Point Pleasant, Cross Creek, Thirteen, Jackson, Red House, Fair Plain, Sandy, New Haven, Wood, and Hartford City. Later, Walton was added.

The salary assessed the district was $425; out of this I had to pay traveling expenses, provide a house to live in, and pay a hired girl. Under such conditions I could afford a house of only three rooms. I never believed in a preacher, or any one else, for that matter, living beyond his income. Debt is an awful devil for the itinerant to contend with, and should be avoided at all hazard. In all the years of my ministry I have never left a pastoral charge or district owing any one thereon a nickel. If a man is fit to be a preacher, debt will distract his mind and put a thorn in his pillow; it cannot be otherwise with a sensitive nature. God save our young men from the habit and curse of debt-making.

No little of my travel, while on the district, was by boat on the Ohio and Big Kanawha rivers. Only one of my fields was touched by a railroad, and that was sixty miles from where I lived. My custom was to go by boat to the point nearest the place of the quarterly meeting, and then walk the remaining distance, whether it be five or twenty-five miles. Often I might have secured conveyance for the asking, but I felt that it was humiliating to be always annoying somebody for favors, nor have I changed an iota in all these years in this regard. If a preacher wants to make himself a nuisance among his parishioners, he can easily do so by constantly making demands upon them which look to his own comfort and that of his family. Many a time I walked from twelve to fifteen miles in a day, held quarterly conference, and preached twice. Occasionally the distance would stretch out to twenty miles. I did not mind the labor so much as I did the suffering from sore feet; walking in the hot sun or over frozen roads, hour after hour, often caused them to blister and bleed. In these experiences I was not alone; many others, some of whom yet live, suffered the same or kindred hardships.

In February of 1879 I was called home to my father's. After a day or two I tried to return, but upon reaching Parkersburg found the river so frozen and clogged with ice that the boats could not run. It was Thursday afternoon. My quarterly was at Oakhill, fully forty miles distant, the next Saturday at two o'clock. The roads were badly frozen and almost impassable. When I saw the situation I determined to make the trip overland as best I could; if I could not find assistance along the way, I would walk it. Leaving the city at four o'clock, I traveled on till darkness overtook me, when I turned aside and knocked at the door of a humble cabin and asked for lodging, which was cheerfully granted; but I had made only a few miles. In addition to the rough roads, I was burdened with a good-sized grip and overcoat. The next morning at daydawn I resumed my journey. Once during the day I rode two or three miles in somebody's sled, but beyond this I got no help. Long after the dinner hour I secured a cold lunch, which the reader may be assured was relished by a tired, hungry man. An hour before sundown I reached Sandyville, where a warm supper was enjoyed at a little hotel. Still I was fifteen miles away from the point for which I was aiming, and felt that I could go no farther without help; but a kind friend generously agreed to loan me his horse to ride as far as Ripley, seat of justice for Jackson County, from which place the mail-carrier was to lead it back the next day; but the poor animal was shoeless, and went crippling along at a snail's gait over the rough ground.

Two miles distant I had to cross Sandy Creek, and found it partly frozen over. It was too dark to discern the danger of fording the stream. After repeated efforts, I succeeded in getting the horse on to the ice, but as quick as a flash it fell broadside, pitching me—I never knew where nor just how far; but the horse beat me up, turned its head homeward, and disappeared in the darkness. What did I do? Well, what almost anybody else would have done under like circumstances. I took the back track and returned to the village where the animal belonged, and found that it had returned in good order. The next morning my feet were so sore that I could not wear my shoes, but was fortunate in securing a pair of arctics in which to travel the rest of the journey. By noon Ripley was reached, where conveyance was secured which enabled me to make the place of meeting and call the conference on schedule time.

Some one may suggest that I was foolish for making such an effort to reach the quarterly when nothing apparently unusual was at stake; maybe I was, but such was my way of doing. I always believed that a preacher ought to fill his engagements promptly unless providentially hindered, and then he ought to be fair enough not to blame providence with too much; but few days are ever too cold and stormy, or nights too dark to keep a man from his appointments if he is anxious to preach the word and minister to his people. I here record the fact, with feelings of satisfaction and pride, that in more than a third of a century I have not disappointed a dozen congregations. As I see it, a preacher succeeds in his work just as business or other professional men succeed in their respective callings. He must bestir himself, and permit no obstacle to get between him and duty; any other policy means failure. At it everywhere and all the time, and keeping everybody else at work, are the only ways to win for the Church and maintain a good conscience before God.

Conference met in Hartford City. The chart showed that a good year had been enjoyed, 1,354 new members being reported. Of this number, 535 were credited to West Columbia District.

The second year on the district was like unto the first—full of toil, responsibility, and peril betimes.

As an indication of what was required of a presiding elder in order to aid his pastors and keep the work of the district well in hand, I relate the following experience: A rainy winter morning found me on Milton Circuit—the last charge in the southwestern part of the conference. I had an appointment that evening at Cross Creek, thirty-five miles east. The mud in some places was knee deep to my horse, but on and on I traveled, over hills and along meandering streams, sometimes walking myself up and down steep places in order to relieve my weary horse. At last, when it was nearly dark, I halted on the bank of the great Kanawha, opposite the town of Buffalo. But how was I to get across the threatening stream? The ice lay piled in great heaps on either shore; the man who tended the ferry hesitated to come after me when I called to him, but he was given to understand that in some way I must be gotten over. Finally he agreed to make the attempt, and after hard rowing, landed me on the opposite side but below the regular coming-out place, and where the ice was badly gorged. Then the real difficulty of the venture was apparent. We had to get the horse up over the great blocks of ice that lay at the water's edge, and it was to two of us an exciting time; no one can describe it on paper. Holding on to the animal, pulling my best at the bridle-rein all the while, the ferryman pushing with all his might, we finally scrambled over the ice and through narrow passageways until a place of safety was reached. How thankful I felt when it was all over, and how I loved that horse! Doctor Warner used to tell how his faithful horse once swam an angry stream, and that after the shore had been reached in safety he dismounted, put his arms around the neck of his deliverer, kissed his lips, and wept for joy. Itinerating in the early days of the West Virginia Conference meant all this, and sometimes much more.

When I got to the church, two miles farther on, I found the congregation waiting and ready to join in the service. It might be stated, in this connection, that in those days the coming of the "elder" was an extraordinary event, and seldom failed to bring out the entire community.

The following evening I had an engagement to preach at Mount Moriah, still farther east some thirty miles. It rained the day through. A part of the journey I followed a single trail, popularly known as a "hog path." Such a route relieved me somewhat from the mud, but, being in the woods, I could not carry an umbrella over me, hence had to take the rain as it came; but I must not disappoint the people. They had my word for it that I would be there, and the promise must be sacredly kept. It was a little after dark when I caught a glimpse of the lights in the old log church; but, hold! I suddenly found myself up against another serious difficulty—Parchment Creek was out of its banks. There seemed no show for getting over except to plunge in and swim my horse. I hesitated; already wet and cold, I was loath to make the attempt. I would have to carry my saddle-bags on my shoulder if I saved my Bible, hymn-book, and sermons; the water would come to my waist, to say the least. Then another trouble appeared; it was too dark to see the road or landing-place on the opposite side, and I might drift below it with the current and not get out at all. While thus cogitating, I heard some boys talking on the other side as they were going to church. Calling to them, I said, "Boys, can't you in some way help me over the creek?" "Who are you?" was the reply. "I'm the preacher," I answered, "and want to get to the church." After a short consultation among themselves, one of them shouted back, "All right; we'll bring the skiff after you." Soon I heard them push out from the shore, and in a few moments they landed near me. "Now," said one, "you get in here with Bill, and I'll swim your hoss over," and in less time than it takes to pen the happenings, he was in the saddle on his knees and starting for the water. Did he get over safely? Yes, indeed; he entered the stream above the usual place of going in, hence the horse swam, not against the current, but at an angle with it. In every way possible I thanked those boys for their kindness to me, for they had certainly kept me from putting my life in peril. If they are still living and should happen to glance over these pages, they will readily recall the event.

The church was nearly full of people, and I certainly enjoyed preaching to them. The great Father had been graciously with me to guide my ways and to protect my life. How glad I will be if, on the morning of the eternal to-morrow, I shall find that the service that evening helped some soul heavenward!

Rev. W. W. Rymer, over thirty years ago, nearly lost his life in this same region on account of high waters. His horse either could not or would not swim, but plunged furiously when beyond his depth. The heroic itinerant stayed in the saddle as long as he could, but was finally dislodged and went down. In the midst of it all he retained his presence of mind and aimed for the nearest shore, which was not far away. Being unable to swim, he crawled on the bottom a part of the way, and at last found himself where he could stand with his head above the water. The horse, fortunately, came out on the same side. Commenting on the incident, Mr. Rymer says: "After my deliverance, it was clear to me that I had been near death's door, and also near heaven. Two thoughts followed; one was: 'If I had not escaped, I would now be in glory,' and I confess I felt good over the reflection. The other was: 'No, it is better that I got out, for if I had drowned, my parents would have had great sorrow.' I took it all to mean that my work was not yet done, and soon experienced great peace of mind. Almost thirty-one years have come and gone since then, but the ruling purpose of my heart all the while has been to preach Jesus. Before thirty-one years more have rolled around, I shall have gone through death's river—yes, through to the other side, where I shall see my Lord face to face."

Let the reader be assured that there is a profound satisfaction in looking back to those times of trial and suffering, of battle and victory, when the ways of Providence were so plain, and when an unspeakable jay crowned the years of toil and service.

After another ride of twelve miles from Mount Moriah, I reached my home in Cottageville, near the Ohio River. How inexpressibly delightful to be at home again with wife and little ones! What a heavenly place home is when love and sunshine await the itinerant's coming! While he ministers to them, they also minister tenderly to him; such mutual love and helpfulness is to be found nowhere else.

My support for the year consisted of $427.83 in salary and $22.41 in presents. Fifty dollars of this went for house rent, and fully as much more for traveling expenses. Beside these outlays, we kept hired help in the home all the time.

Buckhannon, Upshur Country, was the seat of the next session of the conference. The noble Bishop Glossbrenner was with us in the fullness of the Spirit, and charmed us with the warmth and sweetness of his gospel messages. As recording secretary, I edited a little "daily," which gave the proceedings of the conference. This was the first and last attempt of the kind. Such an arrangement is nice, to be sure, and sounds well when we talk about it, but it always costs more than it is worth. The town papers are usually willing and anxious to report the work.

During the session a most amusing incident took place. A colored brother by the name of Waldo came to me at the noon hour on Thursday, and asked me to marry him that evening at eight o'clock. I said, "Waldo, I cannot grant your request. We have an evening session of conference, and I must be there. However, if you will put it off till nine o'clock, I will be on hand." But to such an arrangement he would not agree. The long-looked-for moment could not be delayed. Eight o'clock was the hour about which clustered the sweetest anticipations of his life. The goal toward which he had striven must be reached and won on schedule time. So, with a twinkle of the eye, characteristic of the negro, he exclaimed: "Good Lawd! the thing's gone too fah now; no putting it off." Of course I had to arrange for another secretary under circumstances so vitally essential to the brother's happiness and welfare. The reason why he chose me to perform the ceremony, he said, was because I had converted him eight years before.

CHAPTER V.

The third year on the district brought the usual routine of duties and hardships. By the help of Brother John Dodds, who gave me fifty dollars, I was enabled to purchase a horse and buggy, paying $125 for the entire outfit. This arrangement relieved me of much walking. The horses and mules occasionally used during the previous years were borrowed or hired. My muleback riding, however, was suddenly broken off by a rather painful incident which occurred one night. Striking a bit of good road, I spurred the animal into a gallop, but something happened; its forelegs seemed to give way, and it turned a complete somersault. With my arms extended, I went on, like a flying-machine, several feet before I struck the ground. The fall nearly killed me. I rolled about in agony for a while before I thought of the mule, but when I was able to get up I observed the treacherous beast leisurely eating grass in the fence corner near by, as if nothing had happened. I never liked a mule after that, and, to the best of my knowledge, have not been on one since.

I never thought it out of place to have a little innocent fun once in a while. "Laugh and grow fat," is an old adage which has more in it than some people suppose. A long, wry face is a poor sign of piety. To assume a look of seriousness, as though religion were made up of clouds and shadows and disappointments, is a false representation of the Christian life. If any person on earth has a right to be cheerful and to smile all over his face, it is the one who honestly endeavors to serve God, and has his eyes throneward all the while. Yes—

"A little nonsense now and then

Is relished by the wisest men."

Certainly, then, there is nothing wrong in those not so wise enjoying it.

One blustery March day, after a long, irksome ride over the hills, I was passing a farm-house where two young lads were chopping wood. Here is an opportunity, I thought, to have a little sport; so, reining in my horse, I called, "Say, boys, can you tell me how far it is to where I want to go?" In an instant one of them replied, "Yes, sir; three lengths of a fool; get off and measure." It was no time to talk back, or to interpose objections to such rudeness with a presiding elder. I had gotten myself into the difficulty, so had to get out as gracefully as possible. Bidding them the time of day, I passed on, descanting in an undertone upon the subject of depravity, and wondering what was to become of the rising generation. Since then I have deemed it wise to approach the average boy somewhat cautiously, as one never knows when or in what direction his gun will go off.

About this time, and perhaps in connection with this trip, I had an amusing experience with a brother who appeared before the quarterly conference for license to preach. When asked to state his views on depravity, he frankly admitted that he did not fully understand the doctrine, but said he believed that man was *"teetotally deprived."* Before the examination was over the conference was clear in its judgment that it could not afford to credential a man who was *deprived* of common sense.

During the year it was my privilege and pleasure to convey the greetings of my conference first to the West Virginia Conference of the Methodist Episcopal Church, and then to the Baptist Association of the State. Both were large, influential bodies, and received with marked cordiality the messenger sent by the United Brethren.

While our people of the conference were loyal, and believed in a robust, aggressive denominationalism, they were free from that narrow, bigoted sectarianism which is so unlike the religion we profess. They were cordial and generous in their treatment of others, and always ready to grasp the hand of fellowship, no matter by whom extended. They believed in *union*, and do yet. As far back as 1870, the following was spread upon the conference minutes:

"WHEREAS, The tendency of the times is toward a more intimate union among the various religious denominations of the country; and, whereas, negotiations are now going on between the Evangelical Association and the United Brethren in Christ, looking toward their union; therefore,

"*Resolved*, That we, as a conference, entertain the idea of such a union most favorably, and hope that it can be effected on terms alike honorable to both denominations."

Bishop Glossbrenner again presided at the next session of conference, which convened in Parkersburg. The aggregate salary reported by my district for pastoral support was $2,036, and for the presiding elder, $411.21. The thirty-four pastors in the entire conference received, all told, $6,535, or an average each of $192. Think of it, ye who scan these lines! Men of God working twelve months for a pittance; men of brains and character, of devotion and heroism; think, too, of their families! The wife and mother at home continually, with but few social, or other advantages; the little ones barefooted the year 'round, and sometimes far removed from school and church—all that the husband and father might preach, and win sinners to the Cross. Glorious record, this! the dear Lord has it in his book.

Does some one ask how our men died? Like conquerors. Awhile before conference William H. Diddle, my predecessor on the district, and a comrade in toil, was called to the heavenly home. The end was beautiful, and found his soul in rapture. When far out in the river he shouted back, "Do not be excited. If this is death, I am not afraid to die." His life had been as pure as a sunbeam. His unselfishness was a marvel to many. He literally gave himself for the good of others, and thus became one with his divine Christ, both in sacrifice and service. As he entered the gates I think Jesus said: "Stand back, Gabriel; stand back, Michael; stand back, all ye angelic hosts, and make room for one who must be next only to myself." What a change from a poor, three-hundred-dollar circuit!

For the fourth time I was sent back to the district, but I returned with the feeling that this must be the last year. In my report to conference I had asked to be relieved from district work, but the brethren did not see fit to grant the request.

I am, and always have been opposed to long terms of office. The duties entailed by positions of trust usually are such as to interfere with systematic study. This is the main reason why many officials narrow down in their pulpit work to a few sermons. They do not have time to prepare new discourses. Then there is a tendency among those who hold office, whether in the annual conference or general Church, to develope a spirit of bossism, which is incompatible with United Brethrenism. Perhaps the men in office are not so much at fault as is the system which keeps them there. They somehow get the notion that they must have a finger in everything, and that nothing can be done exactly right without them. There may be, and are notable exceptions, of course, but they are few and widely separated.

Having been elected to the General Conference, with Z. Warner and E. Harper as associates, I attended the meeting of that body which occurred in Lisbon, Iowa, the following May. This was all new to me, but the conference was hardly so interesting as were the vast prairies of Illinois and Iowa, and the marvelous products of the great farms to be seen on every hand. In feeding our horses and cattle in West Virginia, we almost invariably allotted to each just so many ears of corn. Even the swine we expected to butcher were given a daily allowance; but in Iowa I was surprised to see chickens, hogs, cattle, and everything else given free access to the compile. But such is their way of doing out West. The rich soil is transmuted into corn, the corn into pork and beef, and these into gold, which has developed on the material side a wonderful country.

During each of the four years I spent on the district, we held a ministerial institute. This portable school of the prophets was suggested by Rev. E. Harper, now a presiding elder in North Nebraska, as far back as 1875. A whole week at a time would be spent in hearing recitations and lectures, and the work was most thorough. Our studies embraced Old and New Testament history, systematic theology, Christian ethics, homiletics, church history, mental and moral philosophy, English grammar, the English Bible, etc. Some of the textbooks used were gone through again and again in the course of a few years. We used charts, maps, the blackboard—in fact, everything that would aid in the study of the Word, quicken a desire for knowledge, and increase the preacher's efficiency in the pulpit. Dr. Warner was at first our main preceptor; and what a teacher he was! thorough, clear, and enthusiastic; he knew what he wanted to say, and how to say it. He was mighty in the Scriptures; and as a pulpiteer and platform speaker had no equal in his conference, and perhaps nowhere else in the Church. Later, others took part in the work of instruction, which greatly pleased him, relieving him of much of the burden assumed in the outset.

A resolution was adopted to the effect that any preacher who wilfully absented himself from these gatherings, designed especially for his mental and moral improvement, should be left without work until all others had been employed. This policy was drastic, to be sure, but in the end it proved a blessing to our ministry. Much of the clerical material we had on hand was exceedingly raw, but genuine, nevertheless, and susceptible of being wrought into a highly-finished and useful product. One young brother affirmed, publicly, that the crucifixion occurred seventy years before the flood; another, in preaching on Daniel in the lion's den, said he didn't know how he got to Babylon unless he had been shipwrecked. Both of these were good men, and one of them proved very successful as an itinerant. Cases of such dense ignorance were rare, of course, but to such brethren the institute was of incalculable value, as history, geography, chronology, and other features of biblical study were made a specially. But let no one be deceived into thinking that all, or a majority were illiterates. Far from it Some were giants in the pulpit, and were heard with gladness by the multitudes. One after another, other conferences took up the institute idea, until it prevails to-day in one form or another in nearly all the conferences, and no doubt will remain a permanent fixture in the methods of the Church. The plan is a good one, and commends itself especially to young men who are striving for self-improvement in the pulpit, and along lines of practical work. However, before the institute should come the *college* and *seminary*. At a time like the present, when money is abundant, and the beneficiary aid of the church may be drawn upon, every one looking toward the ministry should seek and secure the help proffered by these great institutions. The character and mission of any denomination depend upon the type of its preachers. The United Brethren Church is no exception to this rule.

Grafton was the seat of the next conference, Bishop J. Dickson directing its business. The year had been fairly successful in various ways, but the salaries remained exceedingly low. Over the conference they average $202.88. My own was $433.18, with the addition of $74.50 in presents. Of the thirty-seven charges reported, only two paid as much as $400; five paid from $300 to $350; eleven from $200 to $300; while all the rest fell below $200. But the brethren were ready and willing to try it again. The secretary says at the close of the proceedings: "The unanimity among the preachers and delegates, and the deep solicitude manifested by all for the prosperity of the conference, made the entire session remarkably pleasant." Referring to the Sabbath evening service, he adds: "At the close a number of the ministers made brief remarks relative to their past hardships, and bespoke the prayers of the conference for success during the coming year. This part of the service was deeply affecting." Yes, I remember the occasion well. Dr. Landis, of the Seminary, was present, and wept with the rest of us, as he listened to the story of more than one who was willing to "endure hardness as a good soldier of Jesus Christ."

The following will indicate the courageous attitude of the conference on questions of moral reform:

"WHEREAS, the use of tobacco is expensive, filthy, unnecessary, and, therefore, an evil, and,

"WHEREAS, it is especially unbecoming for ministers of the gospel to surrender to an acquired appetite, defile the body, the temple of the Holy Ghost, and thus, by example, encourage the young to do likewise; and,

"WHEREAS, this evil cannot be remedied so long as ministers freely and openly indulge in it, therefore,

"*Resolved*, 1. That from this time forward no person be granted license to preach by this Annual Conference who persists in the use of tobacco.

"*Resolved*, 2. That all licentiates who indulge this habit be required to give it up before taking upon themselves the vows of ordination."

The significance of this action will be more fully appreciated when it is understood that West Virginia is a tobacco-producing States and that its use, in one form or another, is pretty general among the people. A report on temperance, which mercilessly arraigned the liquor traffic, and its political abetters, was also adopted. Here is a sentence or two from it: "Believing as we do that prohibition is both humane and holy, we can have no sympathy for a policy, or a Christianity that ignores it at the ballot-box." Men who were willing to work for a pittance, which meant that they and their families were to go scantily fed, and half clothed, all for the sake of redeeming their native

State, could not be expected to condone the offenses of the liquor dealer, or to have decent respect for those who did.

House Where the Bishop First Went to Housekeeping and Where His First Child Was Born, Grafton, W. Va.

The next two years were spent in Parkersburg. During the first we had a blessed revival which continued several weeks; in all, more than seventy joined the Church. But during the second year the work was hindered by circumstances beyond human control. A great sorrow came to our home. By degrees the shadows deepened, until the mother of my three children bade us a final adieu, and pushed out into the unseen. God pity and help the itinerant to whom such an experience comes! But my own mother, now of such precious memory, was ready to take the little ones, and to bestow upon them that wealth of care and love which never fails to enrich the life.

The next year was given to the financial management of the West Virginia Normal and Classical Academy, located at Buckhannon. While the school did excellent work for a few years, it eventually went down for want of material support. In view of the losses and disappointments and alienations caused by its failure, I am not sure that the conference did a wise thing in starting it. Little colleges have their advantages, I grant, but trying to operate one at every crossroads on faith and enthusiasm, is too much of a good thing.

By consent of the conference I agreed to give a few months to the business management and associate editorship of the *West Virginia Freeman*, the State prohibition organ. During this period I made a partial canvass of the State in the interest of a prohibition amendment then pending. It would require a whole chapter to tell of my experiences with the old political partisans, some of whom fairly went into spasms at the very mention of prohibition. Our presidential candidate, John P. St. John, had defeated James G. Blaine, so the Republicans affirmed; hence they were ready to vote against anything, or anybody, the angel Gabriel not excepted, who believed on any point as St. John did. Many of these were Christians, so-called, and some of them members of my own Church. I knew them well; and be it said to their everlasting shame, that they went against the amendment, just as did every whiskyite in the State.

Under our system of government the ballot has in it a moral element, and therefore will meet us at the bar of final reckoning. It not only has to do with our political, industrial, and educational affairs, but with the church and family as well. What show will a man have at the last day whose ballot has constantly belied his profession as a Christian? I have never been able to understand how he could enthrone his Lord in the affairs of state by voting a ticket perfectly satisfactory to the drunkard-maker. It remains for an allwise God to determine what disposition shall be made of these vicious ballots when the judgment day comes. Personally, I have no respect for, or confidence in any United Brethren or member of any other church who, knowingly, votes for a man for any office who is opposed to my Christ and the cause for which he stands.

Being ever ready to "speak my piece" against the saloon and its allies, I was constantly stirring up a "hornet's nest" over the business. When I spoke against it, whether in public or private, I never hesitated to pay my respects to the machine politician, since I regarded him and rum as closely related. As the result, some of the newspapers and office-seekers got after me with a vengeance. This I confess was to my liking, since I felt sure I was making at least some kind of impression upon them. Then it gave me a chance to answer their criticisms, and puncture their fallacies. The following extract from one of my replies may be of interest to the reader. The principle laid down will always hold good:

"All at once the saloonist and politician are becoming greatly concerned over the question of 'pure and undefiled religion'; and well they may, for if religion is effectually taken into politics they will as certainly go out. This they fully understand, hence yell themselves hoarse in trying to divert attention when the pulpit begins to let the light in upon their devilish business. While a man is a minister of the gospel, he is also a citizen in common with other men. The fact that he pays taxes, lives under, and is subject to the laws of our commonwealth, makes him such. Then most assuredly he has the same right as other men to be heard upon great political issues that affect the well-being of his country. If not, why not? Touching all moral and political affairs which have to do with the home, the individual, and the general good of the community, the pulpit has ever stood at the front, and so it ever will, unless it sells out to the saloon.

"The truth is, under a government like ours, presumably Christian, all political questions have a moral phase, and to a greater or less extent involve the question of religion. In other words, every question in politics touches at some point the work of the pulpit, therefore it is right and proper for the minister to discuss before his people, prudently, of course, the moral bearings of all these issues. There is nothing that the liquor ring, and old-line politicians would rather do than to stifle the utterances of the pulpit, for well they know that the molding of sentiment, and the training of the moral forces by which the eternal God proposes to overthrow and dash in pieces their strength, must there begin."

In May of this year, 1885, I attended my second General Conference, which met at Fostoria, Ohio, in company with Z. Warner, E. Harper, and S. J. Graham. The occasion was an historic one. Radicalism was given a black eye; the forces of the Church were realigned, and the clouds which had so long hung over our Zion were pierced by the sunlight of a new day.

CHAPTER VI.

The time of holding the annual conference having been changed from spring to fall, the next session was held at the Simmons' chapel, in Lewis County. I was again made presiding elder, stationed on Parkersburg District, and soon moved to Pennsboro, where my headquarters remained for the next four years. My diocese extended from Parkersburg to Irondale, a distance, east and west, of one hundred and sixteen miles, and from the Ohio River on the north far interior to the south. The fields embraced were Parkersburg Station, Parkersburg Circuit, Volcano, Pennsboro, Troy, Middle Island, Littles Mills, Grafton, Irondale, Hessville, Tanner, Sylvan Mills, and Smithton.

A vast amount of hard work, I soon discovered, would be necessary to make anything like a commendable showing in a territory so large and difficult to cultivate. The first duty with me was to care for my preachers. It was my notion then, and my views have not changed in all these years, that if a presiding elder wants his men to do good work he must, first of all, do his best for them financially. If the salary was insufficient, and it nearly always was, as I have shown many times over, it had to be supplemented in one way or another. If the stewards were worthless, I asked them to resign. If they did not know how to collect, I went along and instructed them as best I could. In some cases we would canvass the entire neighborhood with a two-horse team and wagon, and gather up flour, corn, potatoes, chickens, meat, eggs, sorghum, butter—in a word, anything and everything that could be used at the parsonage, or exchanged for groceries. When nothing better could be done, I would load up my own horse with flour and meat and lead him to the preacher's home with his precious cargo of provisions. Then what a good time we would have! Some who are yet at work in the conference were helped in this way. I also found it profitable to have the people on each field, if at all possible, make the pastor a present of a new suit of clothes each year. The plan is usually a popular one, and in most cases can be worked, if placed in the hands of the right persons. It is the equivalent of just so much extra cash to the preacher. But with some it may be a query as to how I managed the indifferent pastor. Sometimes one way, and sometimes another. Every presiding elder, I suppose, has his own methods. My plan was first to aid and encourage him all I possibly could. I tried to prove to him, in a substantial way, that I was his friend, and wanted to help him make his work a success. If, after all this, he persisted in being a failure, I frankly told him he would have to drop out. Such a step requires courage, I know, but it must be taken once in a while. No railroad company or any other business concern would think of employing inefficient, untrustworthy men; such a policy would be suicidal; nor can an elder afford to supply his fields with those who are utterly devoid of fitness for a work so high and responsible.

A man may be a "good fellow" in many respects, and promise to support his elder if continued in active service, but these things should have no weight in the matter of appointments. The welfare of the church should always be considered before that of the individual. If either must go down, let it be the preacher. Why put him in a position to chill, discourage, and perhaps wreck a whole charge? Nor should a man be employed if inefficient by reason of age or poor health. The fact that a minister was once successful is no reason for continuing him indefinitely in the pastorate. A record of usefulness, I know, is a crown of glory to any old, worn-out toiler, but with such glory he ought to be satisfied. I have always hoped, and still do, that I may have sense and grace enough to retire of my own accord before my conference is compelled to put me on the shelf. The church, however, should provide a comfortable living for her servants when they can no longer remain at the front. They deserve such recognition, and to withhold it is to sin against them and the God whose they are, and whom they have served.

With reference to the presiding elder, or superintendent, I will further say that he is the most useful and important man we have if he does his duty faithfully; otherwise he is the biggest bore in the church. He is not a success if he does mere routine work and nothing more. He must reach out. He must be larger than his district, yet strive all the while to make it as big as himself. He must keep things going. If resourceful, he will always find a way to inspire and profit his men, if there is anything in them to respond to his efforts. If he is not a general, he is not fit for the place. He must go panoplied with helmet and breast-plate, shield and sword, ready to fight, preach, or die, on a moment's notice. How the church and pastor are to be pitied when compelled to suffer three or four official visits during the year from an old, dry stick, destitute of sympathy and enthusiasm.

The year was not without its incidents, both serious and amusing. During one of my quarterlies held in the Big Fishing Creek region a fight occurred among some of the toughs as they went from church on Saturday evening. In an article to the county paper I took occasion to criticise, rather sharply, such behavior, and emphasized the fact that the officers of law ought to do their duty in all such cases. In fact, the derelict officials were as severely arraigned as were the offending pugilists.

Three months later I was in that section again; after the Sabbath morning services, at Mt. Olive, I went to Laurel, some miles away, to fill an evening appointment. After riding quite a distance along a high ridge, which overlooks all the country around it, I turned down a little ravine which lead to Laurelrun; but suddenly my cogitations were interrupted by a big, burly sixfooter, who knew of my coming and was waiting for me. Stepping in front of my horse, he blurted out, "Are you the feller what wrote that piece in the paper about me?" I replied that I did not know who he was, or what "piece" he referred to. "I'm one of them fighters you wrote about in the *Star*," he said, "but what you writ wasn't true, so I thought I would wait for you here." In the meantime we were both moving slowly down the hill, and he was at my side. If ever I did hard, double-quick thinking, it was then. I knew what he was there for, and a general mix-up seemed inevitable. I at once decided on a policy. I would talk him out of any evil intent he might have, if it were possible to do so; if not, and nothing else would suffice, I would get off my horse and stay with him just as many rounds as I could, with the hope that somebody might come along and help me out, if help was needed. I began to explain how and where I got my information, and how I felt over such unbecoming conduct on the way from divine worship. At this point he interjected the remark that my informant was a liar, using adjectives and expletives which would not look well in print. But I kept on with my speech, using all the eloquence and fervor at my command. I expatiated on the sacredness of worship, and portrayed in the most vivid colors possible the beauty and praiseworthiness of the young man who honors the gospel, and loves and lives in peace with all men. Though there was blood in his eye at the start, I soon observed that I was gaining on him. By and by he began to sanction what I said. It was clear that I had his attention, so I kept on talking something good to him until he finally stopped me as abruptly as when we first met, saying, "Wal, I guess I'le go back. I kinder thought I'd like to ax you about it. Good-by." What a feeling of relief came to me as the fellow disappeared. A scrap, and possibly something worse, had been avoided. I at once decided, however, that the country editor thereafter would have to look elsewhere for information when such brawls occurred. Such a narrow escape from—I did not know what—convinced me that at least in that particular locality the work of a newspaper correspondent was incompatible with that of a presiding elder.

It was on one of my visits to this same field that I made some of our own dear people very cross over a little verse, purely original, which I wrote on the blackboard. Nearly everybody used tobacco in some form. Many of the women were snuff dippers, and smoked the pipe, while nearly all the men either chewed or smoked, or did both. The stanza ran thus:

Who can chew the dirty stuff,

In the sacred place of prayer?

Who can smoke or rub snuff,

And feel that God is there?

Years afterward, I was told that some were still talking about that bit of poetry.

The district paid a salary of $496.53 to the elder. Out of this he paid for house rent and car fare, $110. The thirty-seven pastors of the conference received an average of $140 each. The highest salary, $480, was received by Rev. R. A. Hitt, on Parkersburg Station, $100 of which was put into rent. The good Lord only knows how he managed to keep his family in respectability, entertain his many visitors, and meet other legitimate expenses, on the pittance of $380. And the same query may be raised in the case of nearly all his colaborers; but they somehow succeeded in making ends meet. As one of them expressed it, "When my wife scrapes the bottom of the flour barrel, God always takes notice." "This is the victory that overcometh the world, even our faith." In addition to the aggregate salary received, the "presents" amounted to $1,276.28, or about $34, upon an average, to each pastor. The net increase in the membership of the conference was 564, an excellent showing. But the most vexing problem was financial. Times were hard, money scarce, and the people generally poor. Yet we believed and wrought in expectation of larger things. Thank God, they are coming.

Pennsboro was the seat of the next conference session. Bishop Weaver presided. Perhaps the most striking event of the occasion was the presence of Dr. Lewis Davis, of Union Biblical Seminary. It was his first appearance among us. Probably the wide difference between his views and those of the conference on the secrecy question had kept him from making an earlier visit; but his presence was highly appreciated by us all, and in turn he greatly enjoyed the courtesies accorded him by the brethren. As I bade him good-by at the train, he said, "Didn't we have a glorious time? I am glad I came. Wish I had come long ago."

The second year on the district was more trying and laborious than the first. The preacher placed in charge of Volcano Circuit resigned before the holidays, and not being able to secure a suitable supply, I decided to keep up the work myself in connection with the duties of the district. The nearest point was ten miles from my home, and the farthest twenty-five; this gave me seven preaching-places; namely, Zion, Volcano, St. Paul, Long Run, Big Run, Harmony Grove, and Freeport. I could give the charge only an occasional Sabbath, hence was compelled to do my preaching and visiting among the people on week days. I held three revivals, preached eighty-three sermons, and collected all the conference benevolences; for this extra service I received $150. Serving as pastor and presiding elder both, kept me from home nearly all the time. It was no uncommon thing to reach home late at night, and then leave early the next morning; but to work was a pleasure and joy; I did not mind the loss of sleep. There was not enough terror in the storm, or "warring elements," to prevent the filling of my engagements. No day was too cold, or night too dark to travel, if, by so doing something could be done toward lifting up the district. I hope there is no egotism in what I here say. *There is none.* I simply state the facts. I lay no claim to superior devotion over my brethren who worked at my side, and were loyal to the core. No others but brave, true men can succeed among the mountains, or anywhere else for that matter; but in some places more faith and courage and sacrifice are necessary than in others.

How I pitied my family. They were alone almost constantly year in and year out. Under such circumstances it was impossible for me to know my children well, or for them to know their father. This statement may be a revelation to many. If any are in doubt as to its correctness, let them ask the opinion of those who have done district work for years at a time.

I never left home without first commending my loved ones to the care of the sleepless Eye; nor did I at any time while absent forget them in my devotions.

Too much cannot be said for the faithful wife of the itinerant. But alas! her worth, I fear, is not appreciated by the church as it deserves to be. People watch and criticise her, to be sure, as they do but few other women, but as a rule she is not accorded a very large place in the achievements of her husband. Indeed, I sometimes fear the minister himself does not realize her true relation to his success in soul-winning. God only knows her anxiety and heart-yearnings as she struggles with the problems of the home in the absence of her husband. What a care the children are to her! But she toils on, as best she can with the means, sometimes sadly limited, at her command.

The fact is, many a successful preacher to-day would be out of the work but for his devoted wife. When ready to quit, and turn aside to some other occupation more lucrative, she put her womanly heart up against his, and urged him on to duty.

Said one of these noble helpers: "Husband, I know we are poor. Our carpets are old and faded, and our furniture is scant and plain. I know our dear children are barefooted, and can't go to school; but I want you to keep on preaching." With a faith unfaltering, and a courage invincible, she was willing to stay in the field—ready to serve, ready to sacrifice, ready to die, and, thank God, ready for heaven.

Her interest in her husband, God's servant, knows no abatement. Day and night she is before the throne in his behalf; and are not her petitions heard? If not, whose will be? We must not deceive ourselves. She has a divinely-appointed place in the work of redemption, and one of tremendous significance—*a helper in soul-saving.* Her reward is sure. As she stands by her husband's side on coronation morning, she, too, will hear heaven's "well done" for the loyal, royal part she has taken, and the service she has rendered in the "ministry of reconciliation."

In the earlier days of the conference, district work was exceedingly laborious, because of the vast mountainous territory to be traversed. If some of the circuits embraced from ten to twenty appointments, extending over portions of three or four counties, it is evident that the presiding elder had his hands full in superintending twelve or fifteen of these fields. The journeys on horseback were long and fatiguing; it was no uncommon thing to change horses at the end of a twenty-five mile ride through the mud, or over the frozen roads. In the midst of one of these long trips, Dr. Warner once stopped a few minutes in Pennsboro, at the home of Mrs. Caroline Sigler, one of God's jewels, and after putting his tired animal away, mounted a fresh one and started on toward his appointment, eating a piece of cold corn-bread. As the good woman looked after him she could not keep the tears back. She knew something of the hardships which had fallen to his lot; yet those hardships were borne with a martyr's courage for the sake of the Church he loved, and in which he died.

On a certain Friday morning I was to leave for my second quarterly on Littles Mills charge, a circuit with which the reader is already familiar because of the happenings I have related in connection with it. The distance was some thirty-five miles. The day brought with it a fearful snow-storm, which seemed to make it unwise for me to attempt the trip on horseback; but I meant to hold the meeting. Wife and children said, "Don't go this time." Others interjected: "You are foolish. Nobody will expect you." But they were mistaken. The people did look for me. Taking the train in the evening I went to Parkersburg, forty miles, and the next day to New Martinsville, fifty-seven miles, and then walked sixteen miles, partly Saturday evening, and the balance of the way the next morning, arriving in time for the 10:30 services. I was glad I went The pastor needed me, and anxiously awaited my coming. I should never have felt right over the matter if I had disappointed him.

CHAPTER VII.

In the days of which I write, a quarterly meeting was a great event, and to many it was a rare privilege to see and hear the "elder." During the summer and fall, especially, the attendance in many instances would be immense. Not unfrequently the women and children present would more than fill the house, which made it necessary to seek a "shady bower," if one could be found. If convenient, the seats were removed from the church and used in the grove, but often this could not be done. More than once I have backed up against a tree, or mounted a log, and preached to a crowd scattered over a quarter acre of ground. On one of these occasions a young girl, of fifteen summers, perhaps, but large for her age, went to a house nearby and got a bucket of fresh water, and bringing it to me in the midst of my discourse, asked me if I would have a drink. I paused long enough to accept the courtesy, and, after thanking her for her thoughtfulness and kindness, continued my talk. Such an infraction of the rules governing divine worship to-day in many sections would greatly amuse the people, no doubt, and perhaps greatly annoy the preacher; but it was seldom noticed by speaker or congregation a third of a century ago among the mountains. When there was no grove near, or the atmosphere was too chilly, or the ground too damp to hold out-door services, we were sometimes sorely defeated by the crowds that came. I here give in full an article which I furnished the *Telescope* on the peculiar provocations of the elder:

"To be a presiding elder in the Parkersburg Conference means to travel over a large territory, and to do a vast amount of hard work on small pay; but all this is nothing compared with some other things that we have to endure. It is no uncommon thing in this country for a presiding elder to make a failure in the pulpit because of some circumstance, or a combination of circumstances over which he can have but little or no control.

"Many of the houses in which we worship are by far too small to accommodate the congregations that generally gather on quarterly meeting occasion. Indeed, many of our meetings are held in schoolhouses, only intended to seat fifty or seventy-five scholars. Now put two hundred persons, or more, into such a space, standing the most of them around the wall, and in the aisles, and then distribute from fifty to one hundred around the house on the outside, each striving to get his head in at a window, and any one, though he be unused to such things, can see the difficulty of preaching under such circumstances. If the people listen with interest they must be comfortably situated.

"In many country districts away from the railroad, the time kept by the people varies so materially that it is next to impossible to get them together at the same hour. No two clocks agree, hence the people begin to assemble at ten o'clock in the morning and keep on *assembling* till noon. At the appointed hour the elder announces the first hymn, and then leads in prayer. During these opening exercises, perhaps twenty-five persons have come upon the ground, and as soon as the *amen* is heard they make a rush for seats.

"Another hymn is sung, and still they come. The text is finally announced, but what of it? The people keep on coming. The middle of the sermon, by and by, is reached, and the preacher is still annoyed; not for three minutes at any time has he had an open field. Only one more proposition to discuss; it is the most important one. His strength has been reserved mainly for it; but just as he begins to lay it open, having secured the attention of the audience, the door creaks and in come a half dozen women. A general stir follows. The seats are all full; something must be done, so a half dozen men get up and surrender their places. Still the people come. The preacher is on the home stretch, but is badly disheartened. He has preached to the people, to be sure, but a good part of the time to the backs of their heads. Not half of those present when he began can tell what his text is. Indeed, he is so confused sometimes that he hardly knows himself what it is. He has just one more illustration to give. He hopes to make it tell, and is succeeding well. The audience for a moment is silent as death; but of a sudden the door opens again and a few more try to enter. In an instant every eye is turned, and the thread of thought is dropped, and the preacher sits down disgusted and dissatisfied.

"Of course it is not always this way, but frequently such is the case. On such occasions the people go home no wiser than when they came. Having been to *meetin'* is the only pleasing thought enjoyed.

"Too many dogs go to church. I am not much of a friend to the canine race at home, much less at church. Dogs piously inclined are the meanest dogs in existence. If they would go under the house or even under the benches in the house, it would not matter so much, but they will not do that. They walk up and down the aisle, and dare even to enter the pulpit where the presiding elder is. All this attracts attention, and detracts from the sermon. Once in a while a dog fight occurs during service, and two or three men have to interfere to adjust the difficulty. If the elder intimates that the congregation or neighborhood is a little too *doggish* to suit him, somebody gets mad and calls him a 'stuck up' sort of a man. 'Beware of dogs,' said Paul. Many a good sermon has been spoiled by them. In West Virginia, especially, they are disturbing elements. I would favor a war of extermination.

"But things are much better with us now than they were twenty-five years ago. We have larger and better houses of worship, and fewer dogs in proportion to population. We expect a great improvement in the next quarter of a century."

It was not an uncommon thing to see a glorious revival start at the quarterly meeting. The love-feast, which almost invariably occurred on Sunday morning before the sermon, was usually an occasion of deep interest. How the old veterans would talk! How eloquent some of them were in their simplicity! How they relished such spiritual feasts! for such they were; and no wonder they were enjoyed by some, for they had traveled, maybe on foot, twenty miles or more to get there. To such the day was a veritable Pentecost. Sometimes in the midst of the sermon or sacramental service, "hallelujahs" would be heard. Yes, once in a while the people shouted, and nobody objected to the noise or excitement. I am no prophet, but will risk the statement that when the church gets so far along that no more hosannah's are heard, it will be about time to reconstruct things and start anew.

A red-hot testimony-meeting in many of our city churches, on the quarterly communion occasion, would make the recurrence of the day and the coming of the elder an event of greater significance than it seems to be at present. Such a service would doubtless lubricate the machinery of the church, and make the work go better. The present plan of enlarging districts has its commendatory features, to be sure, and in some respects it works well, yet the old *régime*, which made it possible for the elder to be present at all the quarterlies, had its advantages.

A word here respecting the genuine hospitality of the people might not be out of place; this, however, is characteristic of Southerners. The presiding elder was not compelled to put up with the pastor all the time because nobody else wanted or invited him; far from it. A half dozen or more at a time would claim him as their guest. Instead of wondering where he would or could go, he was puzzled to know which of the many invitations to accept. How it embarrasses a man to be in a neighborhood where no one seems to want him. Or, if entertainment is proffered he may be further embarrassed by a question mark at the end of the invitation, "Well, are you going with me?" or, "If you've no place else to go, come with us." I have been chilled many, many times since leaving the mountain State by just such half-hearted treatment.

Nor were the presiding elder's official duties performed without an occasional break caused by a wag or ignoramus. Rev. G. W. Weekley was traveling a circuit in Gilmer County with Rev. E. Harper as his elder. At a certain meeting the latter was presiding with his usual grace and dignity while the pastor, being a stickler for law, was making the Discipline the rule of his business conduct. A young man was before them for license to preach. He seemed to be all right, and had made a favorable impression upon his pastor.

"You will please state before the chair and conference," said the pastor to the applicant, "what your reasons are for desiring permission to preach the gospel." In an instant the young brother was on his feet. The question was easy, he thought, and so his answer was clear-cut. "Well," he said, "I always had a desire to see the country, and I thought that being a preacher would give me a chance to do so."

Then it was that the elder wilted and the preacher collapsed, and the quarterly conference looked blank, while the dear young brother felt himself the hero of the occasion.

We met at the Bethel church in Mason County, in September of 1887, to make reports and to review the work of another year. Bishop Kephart was with us for the first, and Dr. Warner for the last time. To show our appreciation of Dr. Warner, the conference gave him a purse containing $25.00 in silver. My district paid, in salary and presents, $526.20, out of which $153 was expended for rent and car fare; 3,720 miles had been traveled by rail, 941 on horseback, and 415 on foot. The average salary in the conference was a fraction over $200. Including "presents," which were considerable in some cases, only one charge, Parkersburg Station, went above $500. One other, Pennsboro, reached $400; eight got above $300, while seventeen paid less than $200 each. The financial report generally was much better than that of the previous year. The aggregate increase in ministerial support on Parkersburg District was $600. Slowly but surely we were pushing ahead and making progress, but at a cost known only to those who were on the field.

The third year on the district was similar to the preceding one, fraught with toil and responsibilities, but not without its spicery, which often did much to enliven the routine work required. One of the first things I did was to secure a horse and buggy. By using the carriage when the roads would admit of it I relieved myself of a good deal of horseback riding. During the winter and early spring no sort of vehicle could be used because of the bad, and sometimes dangerous condition of the public thoroughfares. Nor is the situation in this respect very much different at present from what it was forty years ago. Great changes have been wrought in other regards, but the roads, for the most part, remain the same, and will so continue through the centuries to come.

I had a somewhat provoking experience, once upon a time, as I journeyed with my uncle from Troy to West Union, a distance of twenty-five miles. As the roads were exceedingly muddy I was concerned more than usual about a new suit I was wearing, having pinned the skirts of my clerical coat around my waist in order to keep them clean. We finally struck a place where the thin mud was half knee-deep to the horses. Midway in this mud-hole was a good-sized rock, but not being visible, my steed stumbled over it onto his knees, running his nose into the mud up to the eyes. When he went down I went over his head, and into the puddle face foremost. Fearing that the animal would get on me, I suddenly rolled over and then bounded to my feet. What a picture I presented! I am sure I was no subject for artist or poet. My sleeves were full of mud and water to the elbows, my hat and umbrella both were submerged, and, to add to my chagrin, when I looked up at my uncle, from whom I had a right to expect at least a little sympathy, he was lying over on his horse's neck laughing his best. Going to a stream nearby, I took off my coat and plunged it into the water many times over, much like washing and wringing a bed quilt, until the worst of the mud was off. But such an experience was a mere incident with a mountaineer. When my clothes got dry and the mud was brushed off they seemed to be all right, and I went on with my work just as though the awful mix-up had not occurred.

During the year a great sorrow came to the conference. On the 24th of January the news was flashed over the wires that Doctor Warner was dead. In the next week's *Telescope* "Delta" referred to the sad event as follows:

"The announcement of Dr. Warner's death has cast a deep sadness over the conference. No other conference can feel his loss as we feel it. In a peculiar sense he was ours. No man ever had the hold upon our preachers that he had. We can scarcely realize that he has gone from us to return no more. He may have made mistakes in some things, like other men, but he was a good man. That his soul during his last earthly hours should he 'wonderfully filled with the peace of God,' is just what we might have expected. For thirty years he endured the hardships of a West Virginia itinerant, sometimes traveling day and night, and making the greatest sacrifices to build up the church he loved. Naught but devotion to God's cause ever led him to do so much for it. But his work now is done. Perhaps we should not grieve over his departure, but we cannot help doing so. The entire conference weeps. Said a brother, 'Why didn't the Lord take me, and spare Brother Warner?' This expression serves to show how keenly his loss is felt."

Bishop N. Castle held the next conference at New Haven. During the session I received a telegram that I had been nominated by the prohibitionists of the fourth district for Congress, a compliment which I appreciated all the more because the honor came unsought. Yes, I was a prohibitionist, and am yet, and expect to remain one until something better claims my support. The four hundred votes cast for the ticket in the district represented a thoughtful, moral, courageous element of which I have always been proud. Only such people, as a rule, vote the prohibition ticket. As I entered upon the fourth year of district work I determined it should be my last, at least for a while. I had been kept away from my books already too long, and consciously realized that, while I might be gaining a little some ways, I was losing in others. The church cannot find its highest ideals in men who live wholly outside their libraries. It is study—familiarity with the thoughts and methods of others—that broadens a preacher. The map studied by many of us is too small, and needs to be enlarged so as to extend the vision. If we would see and know things, we must look and search after them. The man is exceedingly unfortunate who, having eyes, refuses to see, and having intelligence, neglects the acquisition of knowledge. My advice to the young man at the threshold of the ministry is, "Buy good books and read them; study your discourses thoroughly and with an eye to somebody's salvation, and then give the people the very best that God has put in you."

This was a good year for the district. As it was to be the last, I determined to make the best record possible for my successor, to duplicate or excel. To succeed meant to go all the time. Distance, bad weather, dangerous roads, swollen streams, or any other circumstances were seldom allowed to get in the way. When Lincoln was asked if he thought the war would close during his administration, he replied, "I don't know, sir, I don't know." "What, then, is your purpose?" was further asked, to which the characteristic answer was given, "Peg away, sir, peg away." It is this, everlasting "pegging away"—forcing one's way through difficulties, and surmounting obstacles—that wins, not only in West Virginia, but everywhere else.

Buxton wrote: "The longer I live the more deeply I am convinced that that which makes the difference between one man and another—between the weak and powerful, the great and insignificant—is *energy*, invincible determination, a purpose once formed, and then victory or death." I quote Buxton's words because they are gold, and have in them the ring of triumph.

TRAVELING A DISTRICT

The year brought its usual harvest of incidents—some serious, others laughable and amusing. It is well to have a streak of fun occasionally flash across our pathway to enliven a journey, or some task to which we have set our hands.

One bleak Monday morning in December I was riding along a high ridge in Wetzel County on my way home from a quarterly just held in that region. To my right a few rods I observed a young man husking corn. He was evidently working his best to keep warm, and, of course, not in a very good condition to be fooled with by a stranger; but I thought I must say something, and run the risk of an explosion. Reining up my horse and getting his attention, I called to him, "Go it; that's the way I got my start." "Yes," he said, with lightning speed, "and a thunderin' start you got," and then made the fodder rattle so that if I had replied he could not have heard me. To be honest, I had not the disposition to talk back, for nothing suggested itself at the moment as an appropriate response; but for the next mile I laughed over the episode and considered myself fortunate that nothing more serious had happened.

I might add that not far from this place Rev. S. J. Graham, years before, suddenly found himself in a kind of menagerie one frosty morning. In those days laymen would frequently make long trips with the preacher or elder; spending several days from home. They thought less about business and more about the church than some do at present. On the occasion referred to, Brother N. Kuykendoll was with the elder. One night they lodged with a friend in his little log cabin of one room. Of course they were well treated and given the best the humble home could afford. Their host arose early next morning and built a fire in an old-fashioned fire-place, which admitted of a "back log" and "fore sticks" before the "kindling" was put in. Soon the shanty was warm. The lay brother awoke first, and, glancing about the room, said to his bed-fellow in a low tone: "Brother Graham, get up; the millennium has come." The preacher raised himself on his elbow and looked, and sure enough there was a strange mixture of animals lying on the hearth before the fire—a pet lamb, a pet pig, a huge dog, and two or three cats. Years afterward I heard these brethren talk and laugh over the experience with as much zest as if it had occurred only the week before.

To indicate something of the work done this year, and that had to be done to carry out the program of a presiding elder, I here insert a few pages of a brief diary which I kept:

January 1, I wrote: "I now begin a new year. God help me. My time, strength, soul—all must be given to the work of the church. With my family I took dinner with Brother C. R. Brown, a precious man."

2.—"Worked on a sermon on coveteousness. Got 'Sweet Sicily' and read it."

3.—"Voted for town corporation officers. Wrote a number of letters. Brother Poling came in the evening, and spent the night with me."

4.—"Worked hard on my sermon on coveteousness."

5.—"Went to Parkersburg in the forenoon, and held business meeting at night. All was pleasant. Lodged with Pastor Martin."

6.—"Preached from 1 Cor. 13:12 in the morning. Good meeting. Audience melted to tears. Attended Sabbath school at 2:30 p. m., conducted the quarterly experience meeting at six, and preached again at 7:30. House full of people."

7.—"Returned home on early train. With wife went to hear Methodist preacher at night."

8.—"At home, studying and answering correspondence."

10.—"Went to Parkersburg again. Dined with Brother J. H. Spence. Assisted in meeting at night."

11.—"With the pastor visited eleven families. Large crowd at evening service."

12.—"Went to Red Hill, six miles distant, and held quarterly at 2:00 p. m. Preached in the evening."

13.—"Preached at 10:30 a. m. from Titus 2:9. Good feeling. Large sacramental service. Shout in the camp. Pastor Devol leaped for joy. Preached again at night."

14.—"Came to the city and returned home. All well."

15.—"In study all day. Attended M. E. Church at night. An interesting revival in progress."

16.—"At home preparing for dedication."

18.—"Left home on early train, and reached Buckhannon at 4:00 p. m. Went to Mt. Washington, eight miles in the country, and preached at night on the 'Prodigal Son.' Thirteen seekers at the altar and four more asked prayers. Lodged with Brother Reese."

19.—"Rode fourteen miles to 'Uncle Jimmy' Hull's for dinner, and then went to Union Hill where I preached at night. Met Elder Graham."

20.—"Rained hard. Congregation small. Raised $85. At night tried it again. Good feeling. Secured $68.50 more and dedicated church. Opposition from another church."

21.—"Rode sixteen miles to Buckhannon through a fearful snow-storm. Went to Weston on train and rode seven miles in the country."

23.—"Returned home. Found all well."

I now turn to the March record because it has to do with one of the sad things which not unfrequently comes to the itinerant.

15.—"I started at noon for Troy Circuit, reached Auburn late in the evening."

16.—"Visited Father Williams and wife. The latter has been in bed three years. Read the Word and prayed with them. Both got happy. Sung a hymn or two for them. Held quarterly at 2 p. m., and preached on 'Stephen, the First Martyr.' A good time."

17.—"Sunday. Held prayer-meeting at 10 a. m., and preached at 11. Large communion. Big shout in the camp. Collection $20. Talked again at night. One of the best quarterlies I ever held."

I pause here. On Monday evening Father Perry came, and preached for us. After returning from church he turned to me and tenderly said, "Now, Brother Weekley, I have a little news for you. As I came through your town this noon I was told that your youngest child was critically ill. The doctor regards her case as dangerous. I would have told you sooner, but I knew it would so trouble you that you could not enjoy the service. I knew also that you would not dare start home in the night, and thus endanger your life. So I waited. Now leave her with God; get what rest you can, and then be off by daylight in the morning." But I got no rest. It was a long, long night of tossing and anxious waiting. At day dawn I started. The muddy roads were frozen over, but not sufficiently to bear up my horse. A part of the time I walked. It seemed I could make no headway at all, and didn't make much in some places. When within two miles of home, I called at a farm-house and inquired if they had heard from my family, and they told me they had not. This brought me relief, for I was sure they would have heard the news if the child were dead. At 1 p. m. I landed safely and found, sure enough, that a blessed Providence had kept the black-winged angel from our home.

How such harrowing experiences try the very soul of the over-worked, half-paid, care-worn man of God, who must spend all his time and strength away from home in some obscure field! They test the material that enters into his composition. To put the Cross and sinful souls before one's own family requires great faith—faith in the Redeemer, faith in his church, and faith in the winning, victorious power of the gospel; and this is what every itinerant in West Virginia had to have.

To indicate the nature and work of our preachers' institute. I return to my diary and give the items of a few days.

July 9.—"At home preparing for institute which meets to-morrow."

10.—"Went to Smithton, and took charge of institute. Rev. H. T. Athey assisted some. Lessons were in Old Testament history and homiletics. Revs. H. T. Athey, H. R. Hess, R. M. Hite, G. A. Davis, J. P. Piggott, and W. H. Albert were present."

11.—"Met at 8 a. m. Recitations. Hess gave a talk on the 'Apocalypse.' Davis preached at 7 p. m. Good sermon."

12.—"Recitations as usual. Davis made an address on 'Prayer.' Good. Hite read a paper on 'Fore-ordination.' Discussed. Piggott preached well at night."

13.—"Recitations as usual. I read a paper on 'Divorce and Adultery.' Also presented a diagram of Solomon's Temple. Hess preached. Good meeting."

14.—"Sunday. I preached at 11 a. m. Large crowd in grove. Good liberty, and good attention. Athey preached at 3:00 p. m., and did well. Returned home."

The records of a few days immediately following may also be of interest.

24.—"Drove with my family to father's, fifteen miles distant."

25.—"Started for Hessville quarterly. Drove thirty-seven miles to Father Mason's."

26.—"Drove to Bee Gum Station fifteen miles further east. Good meeting in afternoon. Preached at night."

27.—"Sunday. Discoursed at 10:30 a. m. on 'The New Testament Church.' Preached again at three o'clock on 'Benevolence and Honesty.' Led song service. Drove fifteen miles back to Brother Mason's."

28.—"Left at 6 a. m. and drove thirty-seven miles to father's."

But it is needless to further reproduce here the jottings made long years ago. The brief memorandum given is but a fair index to the activities of the entire twelve months, or, I might say, to the forty-eight months spent on the district.

CHAPTER VIII.

Buckhannon was again the seat of conference, and was in charge of Bishop Weaver. This was his last visit to West Virginia. My district reported about 600 conversions and accessions to the church. The average salary for the pastors of the conference was $230. After paying house rent and car fare, I had $365.79 left for the support of a family of five, and with which to purchase books, papers, and stationery; but I did not complain; it was more than the average circuit-rider was getting. On this little sum we seemed to live fairly well, and imagined ourselves as respectable as anybody in the town.

In looking over my report, I see at its close the following significant statement: "Now, brethren, suffer a word more. I kindly and earnestly request that you relieve me from district work. Eight years out of the past eleven have been given to this kind of service. While I certainly appreciate what you have done for me, I must say that I am tired of the place, and am anxious that some one else take it. All there is in it, whether money, distinction, responsibility, or hard work, I cheerfully surrender to some one else, with the earnest wish that he may prove more efficient than I have been, and that under his labors enlarged blessings may come to the district."

This was my last year as a presiding elder in the dear old conference.

It is now many years since I was transferred to another field, but almost daily my thoughts go back to my native home, and to the twenty years of unceasing toil given to the building up of the church in that mountainous region. Indeed, I could scarcely get away. It was no easy matter to sever the relations of a life-time. In looking over my brief record of daily happenings I find that July 16, 1889, while pastor at Buckhannon I wrote:

"Received a letter to-day from Rev. C. Wendle, urging me to come to Rock River Conference. Bishop Kephart also writes in like manner. Do not know what to do, but must do right. Lord help me." October 3, I expressed my thoughts and feelings as follows:

"At home trying to pack our goods. What a task it is! Is God in this? I do hope so. It is so hard to leave West Virginia. These hills and valleys all seem sacred to me."

The last time I visited my parents before removing West, I was deeply affected to see how frail they seemed, and thus referred to it: "Parents are getting old. How they are bending beneath the weight of years! Alas, how short life is! Twenty years ago when I left home father had no gray hairs. Now his head is white as wool. Mother! what a faithful soul! How self-sacrificing! Anything to help her children and make herself a blessing to others. Heaven is anxious to get such an angel. May earth keep her yet a long while."

These excerpts from my diary indicate that it cost me something—a heart-struggle, at least, to turn my back upon scenes and associations which were as sacred as life itself. But in making the change I felt I was following the leadings of Providence, and that all would be well in the end.

The fellowship of the brethren I left behind was sweet. Those who looked on were compelled to say, "Behold, how good and how pleasant it is for brethren to dwell together in unity." There was as little jealousy and self-seeking and rivalry in the conference as I ever found anywhere. We all were poor, and could sing like the old Methodist pioneer on his four weeks' circuit:

"No foot of land do I possess,

No cottage in the wilderness;

A poor wayfaring man,

I lodge awhile in tents below;

Or gladly wander to and fro,

Till I my Canaan gain.

"Nothing on earth I call my own;

A stranger to the world unknown,

I all their goods despise;

I trample on their whole delight,

And seek a country out of sight,

A country in the skies.

"There is my house and portion fair;

My treasure and my heart are there,

And my abiding home;

For me my elder brethren stay,

And angels beckon me away,

And Jesus bids me come."

There was another verse we all cherished, and often sung it, as it seemed so appropriate:

> "A tent or a cottage, why should I care?
>
> They're building a palace for me over there;
>
> Though exiled from home, yet still I may sing,
>
> 'All glory to God, I'm the child of a King.'"

In all my travels throughout the Church I have never found any conference that could sing as the West Virginians did. Diddle, Harper, Graham, Orr, Hitt, Holden, and Wood were among the earlier men. Later their places were taken by Cunningham, Piggott, Sallaz, Slaughter, Carder, and Robinson. But it is hardly fair to name a few. All could sing; and so they can to-day.

Singing was an inspiring feature of every conference gathering. It made the air electric, and caused high voltage pressure. We would sing on the train, on the boat, at the hotel—everywhere. On our way from conference, in 1879, we all stopped at a hotel in Weston for dinner. As usual, the singers were lined up in a little while, and fairly shook the old inn with some of their latest and freshest selections. Before we quit, the town was thoroughly stirred up. People left their business places and came to listen. Women and children stood in the doors of their homes, or looked out at the windows, and wondered what it all meant. Two young men, some blocks away, heard the singing and started on a run for the hotel. As they passed some parties one of them was heard to say, "I'll bet five hundred dollars they are Brethren preachers."

Professor Diddle, assisted by others, published the *West Virginia Lute* in 1868, which had a tremendous sale, both among our people and those of other churches. Then Baltzell's music, probably *Golden Songs*, came next among our own publications. This was also a popular book, and one of great merit. While it contained many imperfections, it was nevertheless thoroughly "orthodox" from our view-point. The author was not a scientific music writer. He did not grind his songs out at the organ in a mechanical way, but manufactured them in his heart. Such music always takes. There is something about it that gets hold of the soul and stirs its deepest emotions. I do not understand what that something is, but it is there, all the same.

It was a very common remark among the people of other churches: "If you want to hear singing, get a lot of Brethren preachers together." We had no organs or pianos in any of the churches, with skilled performers to lead the audience. To aid in getting the "pitch," a "tunningfork," or horn was used—a clever little device which every leader carried. But few of the brethren, however, understood the grammar of music. They had had no special training—but no difference; they could sing anyhow. They were not poets, but had the poetic touch. I have heard these men of God again and again sing until the audience was fairly entranced, and until the fire of joy was kindled to a flame in their own hearts. They were rivals of Israel's shepherd king, and wrought things more marvelous than he, through the melodies they sang.

While their music was not classical, it seldom failed to strike fire. The people liked it, and were charmed, encouraged, and, in a thousand instances, saved by it. Mr. Alexander, the great revival singer, has the right view of things. He writes: "Musicians often say to me, 'Why do you not use classical music, above the style of gospel songs?' I reply, 'When you can show me similar effects following such high-class music in moving the hearts of men and women, I will use it fast enough. Until then I shall keep to gospel songs, which have a wonderful way of reaching everybody, because they touch the soul.'"

Volume, fervor, soul, enthusiasm, is what we want in all our church music. Away, forever, with that operatic nonsense which the artistic would introduce into our present-day religious services.

What glorious revivals were promoted. Like cyclones they seemed, at times, to lay everything low in their course. How sinners wept and repented! How saints shouted aloud for joy! "Wild fire!" does some one suggest? May be it was; but it achieved wonderful results. The present ministry of the conference, with a great majority of the true and tried laymen who constitute the very backbone of the church, were converted in just such meetings; and it is quite likely that the leading ministers and laymen of every other conference in our Zion were converted under like circumstances. Call it "wild fire" if you will, but I would like to see a good deal more of it.

A revival that arouses a whole community and brings fifty or a hundred, or perhaps two hundred into the kingdom, some of whom become prominent preachers of the word, while others become very pillars in the church, is not to be ignored or decried by those who are too slow and formal and dull to create a stir. Better have a little "wild fire" than no fire at all.

Personally, I believe in excitement. Nothing worth thinking about is ever accomplished in its absence. We cannot relish food, or enjoy sleep, until first excited by hunger or fatigue. Why should not the church manifest as much zeal and enthusiasm in her work as political parties or commercial clubs do in theirs? I am tired of that contemptible sentiment which stands ready, everywhere, and all the time, to denounce everything that has to do with the emotions. Religion, I readily grant, does not consist of noise and bluster. It means vastly more than that. Nor does it consist in sitting around like so many lifeless knots on a log.

We are told that it is the lightning and not thunder that kills. True enough, but lightning in the absence of thunder is harmless. Lightning makes the thunder.

In our work but little was said about the new theology, or higher criticism. Watson and Ralston in their theologies, and Smith and Clark and Lange and Barnes in their expositions, seldom referred to the new-fangled theories which confuse and chill and curse some of the churches to-day. We all believed that Moses wrote the Pentateuch, and Paul the Epistle to the Hebrews; and personally I have never had any reason for changing my views. It had never occurred to us to put Job and Jonah on the fictitious list. We actually believed and preached that they lived and wrought, one in the land of Uz, and the other in Nineveh, after escaping from the whale's belly. We tried to tell of the awfulness of sin, as well as the joys of religion. We believed in a heaven, and would often talk and sing and preach about it until we felt ourselves within its very suburbs. When Jesus said, "And these shall go away into everlasting punishment," we supposed he meant it, and no one attempted to put an artificial bottom in the "bottomless pit." We divided our time pretty well between Sinai and Zion. The decalogue and beatitudes were included, ofttimes, in the framework of the same sermon. We knew there were some inaccuracies in the authorized version, but nothing sufficiently serious to affect the fundamentals of Christianity. We were justified, as we thought, in preaching the whole Bible, as it was commonly understood and interpreted, because in doing so we were blessed and sinners were saved.

The "mourners' bench" was always a part of the program in our revival work. While no one insisted that a man must be saved at the bench, if saved at all, we believed, nevertheless, that coming forward and bowing at the altar was a good way of confessing sin, and of plighting fidelity to Jesus Christ. I would not serve as pastor of a people who objected to the use of an altar. If some of the unsaved wanted to seek their Lord elsewhere, and in some other way, I should not object; but I should insist upon it that those who wanted to come forward for prayers should have the privilege of doing so. It is refreshing to see how simple and direct Dr. Torry, "Billy" Sunday, and "Gipsey" Smith are in their methods, and the wonderful results that follow. They do not mince matters. They go to the people with a burning message from the Throne, and deliver it, no matter what anybody may think or say about it. With sledge-hammer blows they drive it home to the hearts of their hearers, that no man can be saved until he confesses his sins and his Savior. They follow, largely, the old line of revival work—and *succeed*.

The preacher who cannot build a fire in his church is a failure. In no other way can he attract attention. The church of God has been used to fire from the beginning. Moses got a good warming-up before the burning bush on Horeb; so did Elijah, and others, on Carmel. The disciples were not ready to preach or the church to work until a burning Pentecost came, and fire-flakes fell from heaven upon them. We need great revivals, and can have them, if we are willing to pay the price.

One serious hindrance to the work is the fact that too many profess to have found a "new way." They council moderation, and would have us go about the business with that cold, mathematical precision which the astronomer employs in measuring the heavens. As the result, many of our revival efforts turn out to be very *moderate* affairs. They are self-constituted appointees to shut off steam and put down the breaks, and they succeed. What we need is more steam; that is, purpose, push, and power. And I rejoice in the thought that the thing for which we have waited and prayed is at hand. The semi-skepticism and indifference which have so handicapped the work of evangelism in the last twenty-five years, are giving place to larger activities and simpler methods. We are facing the morning light. The reaction and readjustment will bring in a new era of moral and spiritual triumphs in soul-winning.

The church at large knows but little about the excessive labors and sacrifices of the earlier ministry in West Virginia. My heart still weeps as I think of what some of the brethren endured. But, brave souls they were, they did it because they loved the church and her Christ.

Only three or four remain who were in the conference when I joined thirty-seven years ago. Four others—Revs. E. Harper, I. M. Underwood, A. Orr, and Dr. J. L. Hensley—have located in other conferences, but the great majority have gone to heaven. From hillside and mountain-top they ascended to a place of honor by their Lord, to live in the white light of the throne forever.

"Oh, how sweet it will be in that beautiful land,

So free from all sorrow and pain;

With songs on our lips and with harps in our hands,

To meet one another again."

Does any one inquire to know the real secret of their power? It is not easily explained. They had intellectual girth, but this was only incidental to their success. Their surroundings were inspiring, their spirits exuberant, their physical endurance tremendous, their zeal unflagging, but the secret lay deeper; these were only tributary. It seems to me that the one quality which exalted them, and gave them the mastery over men was *reality*. They were *genuine*. God counted them among his captains, and they were loyal to the last. *Duty* and *destiny* were to them overwhelming suggestions. In them were wrapped up the present and the eternal hereafter.

I can still hear Brother Graham singing as he rode through storm and heat, carrying aloft the banners of the church:

> "Above the waves of earthly strife;
>
> Above the ills and cares of life;
>
> Where all is peaceful, bright and fair,
>
> My home is there, my home is there."

Chevaliers, divine!

> "Their burning zeal no langour knew,
>
> For Christ, his cause, his tempted few;
>
> At home, abroad, where'er their lot,
>
> Their much-loved theme they ne'er forgot."

"One soweth and another reapeth," is the divine law. The foundations of the church among the Virginia hills and mountains were laid amid self-givings, known only to Him who gave to his servants their marching orders, and who accompanied them every foot of the way. A better day has come to the conference. The fields of labor have been greatly reduced in size, pastoral support has been improved, educational advantages have been increased, which means so much to the itinerant's family, and in other respects conditions made many-fold better.

The present membership is 15,000 divided among sixty circuits and stations. Two hundred and six church edifices, worth $243,869, are reported, and thirty-eight parsonages valued at $31,939.

The territory embraces four districts. While the number of presiding elders might be diminished, it would not be wise to try the experiment of giving one superintendent charge of the whole conference. The country is too rough, the distances too great, and the public facilities for travel too meager for one man to do it all.

The average salary paid the pastors in 1906 was $379.45, including house rent and special gifts. Three of the charges went to between $800 and $900; one paid from $600 to $650, and eight others over $500 each. The presiding elders averaged $563.97. For all purposes $50,589.49 was collected. These figures show that in spite of the adverse circumstances with which we have had to battle for the last half century, real progress has been made. But more ought to be done in the next fifteen years than has been accomplished in the last fifty.

Some portions of the State are becoming immensely wealthy through the oil and mining industries. Our people are sharing in the general prosperity, and many of them are growing rich. The commercial possibilities of the State are great and promising as its hidden treasures are brought to the surface, and put on the world's market. The work of the present ministry is to broaden the benefactions of our membership by teaching them the true meaning of Christian stewardship and the obligations which it imposes. In proportion as this is done, salaries will be increased more and more, the offerings to the various benevolent societies multiplied, and larger sums provided for Otterbein University and Union Biblical Seminary.

There is quite a stretch of time between the penning of these lines and the day I started for my first circuit. Thirty-seven years is a good while. My experiences have been numerous and varied. The way at times has been rough, the tasks difficult, and the responsibilities great, but, after all, if I had my life to live over *I should spend it in the gospel ministry, and start again in West Virginia.*

Milton Keynes UK
Ingram Content Group UK Ltd.
UKHW030846141124
451205UK00005B/464